BAPTISTWAY®

Adult Bible Study Guide

Exodus

*Freed to
Follow God*

Brian Harbour
Bob Campbell
Ron Lyles

BAPTISTWAY PRESS®
Dallas, Texas

BAPTISTWAY PRESS® Management Team
Executive Director, Baptist General Convention of Texas: Charles Wade
Coordinator, Church Health and Growth Section: H. Lynn Eckeberger
Director, Bible Study/Discipleship Center: Dennis Parrott

Publishing consultant: Ross West, Positive Difference Communications
Cover and Interior Design and Production: Desktop Miracles, Inc.
Cover Photo: Traditional site of Mount Sinai, photo by William H. Stephens

First edition: June 2004
ISBN: 1–931060–48–7

How to Make the Best Use of This Issue

Whether you're the teacher or a student—
1. Start early in the week before your class meets.
2. Overview the study. Review the table of contents and read the study introduction. Try to see how each lesson relates to the overall study.
3. Use your Bible to read and consider prayerfully the Scripture passages for the lesson. (You'll see that each writer has chosen a favorite translation for the lessons in this issue. You're free to use the Bible translation you prefer and compare it with the translation chosen for that unit, of course.)
4. After reading all the Scripture passages in your Bible, then read the writer's comments. The comments are intended to be an aid to your study of the Bible.
5. Read the small articles—"sidebars"—in each lesson. They are intended to provide additional, enrichment information and inspiration and to encourage thought and application.
6. Try to answer for yourself the questions included in each lesson. They're intended to encourage further thought and application, and they can also be used in the class session itself.

If you're the teacher—
A. Do all of the things just mentioned, of course.
B. In the first session of the study, briefly overview the study by identifying with your class the date on which each lesson will be studied. Lead your class to write the date in the table of contents on page 5 and on the first page of each lesson. You might also find it helpful to make and post a chart that indicates the date on which each lesson will be studied. If all of your class has e-mail, send them an e-mail with the dates the lessons will be studied.
C. Get a copy of the *Teaching Guide*, a companion piece to this *Study Guide*. The *Teaching Guide* contains additional Bible comments plus two teaching plans. The teaching plans in the *Teaching Guide* are intended to provide practical, easy-to-use teaching suggestions that will work in your class.

D. After you've studied the Bible passage, the lesson comments, and other material, use the teaching suggestions in the *Teaching Guide* to help you develop your plan for leading your class in studying each lesson.

E. You may want to get the additional adult Bible study comments—*Adult Online Bible Commentary*—by Dr. Jim Denison, pastor of Park Cities Baptist Church, Dallas, Texas, that are available at *www.baptistwaypress.org* and can be downloaded free. An additional teaching plan plus teaching resource items are also available at *www.baptistwaypress.org*.

F. You also may want to get the enrichment teaching help that is provided in the *Baptist Standard*, in either the printed or the internet editions. Call 214–630–4571 to begin your subscription to the *Baptist Standard*. Access the internet information by checking the *Baptist Standard* website at *http://www.baptiststandard.com*. (Other class participants may find this information helpful, too.)

G. Enjoy leading your class in discovering the meaning of the Scripture passages and in applying these passages to their lives.

Exodus: Freed to Follow God

How to Make the Best Use of This Issue   3

Introducing Exodus: Freed to Follow God   7

UNIT ONE

Preparation for Deliverance

Date of Study

LESSON 1   _____   *Just When Things Were Going So . . .*
    Exodus 1:6–10; 1:22—2:15; 2:23–25   13

LESSON 2   _____   *Excuses, Excuses*
    Exodus 3:1–14; 4:1–15   23

UNIT TWO

God's Power to Deliver

LESSON 3   _____   *The Futility of Resisting God*
    Exodus 7:1–6, 14–18; 8:1–3, 16, 20–21;
    9:1–4, 8–9, 22–26; 10:3–6, 21–23, 27–29   35

LESSON 4   _____   *A Night Never to Be Forgotten*
    Exodus 11:1–8; 12:21–32   47

LESSON 5   _____   *Sing to the Lord for Freedom!*
    Exodus 14:21—15:2, 20–21   57

LESSON 6   _____   *No Longer but Not Yet*
    Exodus 15:22—16:7; 17:1–7   67

UNIT THREE

Guidance for Covenant Living

LESSON 7   _____   *Wonderful Offer, Serious Demand*
    Exodus 19:1–12   79

LESSON 8   _____   *Treat God Like This*
    Exodus 20:1–11   87

LESSON 9   _____   *Treat People Like This*
    Exodus 20:12–17   97

LESSON 10 _____ *The Nitty-Gritty of Covenant Living*
Exodus 21:12–17, 22–27;
22:21—23:11   107

U N I T   F O U R

Called to Worship Only God

LESSON 11 _____ *A Broken Covenant and a Second Chance*
Exodus 32:7–34   119

LESSON 12 _____ *Starting Over*
Exodus 34:1–28   129

LESSON 13 _____ *God Dwelling Among Us*
Exodus 25:1–8; 29:43–46;
33:7–11, 14–16; 40:16–38   139

Our Next New Study   151
How to Order More Bible Study Materials   153

Exodus: Freed to Follow God

Why study the Book of Exodus? In addition to the obvious fact that Exodus is part of the Bible, finding an Old Testament book that is more important—and more important for understanding the New Testament—would be challenging.

In a sense, Exodus, not Genesis, is the first book in the Bible. That is, Exodus really comes before Genesis in spite of the fact that Genesis is first in our Bibles. The meaning of that thought—that Exodus comes before Genesis—is that Israel would never have been interested in the message of the first book in the Bible if God had not redeemed them from Egyptian bondage and covenanted with them to be God's people. Indeed, we probably never would have heard of a ragtag group of people called Israel had their redemption from Egyptian bondage at God's hand not occurred. This redemption is described in the Book of Exodus.

Dr. Page Kelley, a great Baptist who also was a great Old Testament scholar, put it succinctly, "The Exodus is to the Old Covenant what the resurrection is to the new."[1] He continued by saying, "Israel herself regarded the Exodus as the most significant event in her history."[2] Such accolades call us to study the book that tells of this significant event.

Our study is organized into four units. The first unit, "Preparation for Deliverance," deals with Exodus 1—4. These chapters begin with an explanation of why the Israelites were in Egypt. They then tell of the oppression the Hebrews were suffering and of God's early provision for bringing them help in spite of the ruthless measures the Egyptian pharaoh took against them. The Scriptures further describe Moses' early life and God's call to Moses, a call that Moses resisted.

The second unit, "God's Power to Deliver," continues with Moses' return to Egypt and confrontation of Pharaoh. Moses delivered the Lord's message, "Let my people go" (Exodus 5:1).[3] When Pharaoh refused, God sent a series of mighty actions called plagues on Egypt. At last, after the terrible night of the tenth plague, commemorated by the Hebrews in the institution of Passover, Pharaoh did let the Hebrews go.

Pharaoh, though, was not through with the Hebrews. Pharaoh and his army came after them. God, however, was not through with Pharaoh. God miraculously delivered the Hebrews from certain destruction. He "turned the sea into dry land," and "the Israelites went into the sea on dry ground" (Ex. 14:21–22). When the Israelites were safe, God sent the waters back to their normal condition. "The waters returned and covered the chariots and the chariot drivers, the entire army of Pharaoh that had followed them into the sea" (14:28). God continued to provide for the Israelites in the wilderness, although they grumbled and looked back to the good old days of oppression. The background Scriptures for unit two are from Exodus 5—18.

Unit three, "Guidance for Covenant Living," deals with background Scripture passages from Exodus 19 through Exodus 24. The unit begins with a lesson on God's making the covenant with the Israelites. It continues with lessons on the Ten Commandments and the detailed laws often called the covenant code or the "book of the covenant" (24:7).

Additional Resources for Studying the Book of Exodus:[4]

Walter Brueggemann. "Exodus." *The New Interpreter's Bible*. Volume 1. Nashville: Abingdon Press, 1994.

Joy Davidman. *Smoke on the Mountain: An Interpretation of the Ten Commandments*. Philadelphia: The Westminster Press, 1953; reissued by Westminster John Knox Press, 1985.

Maxie D. Dunnam. *Exodus*. The Communicator's Commentary. Volume 2. Waco, Texas: Word Books, Publisher, 1987.

John I. Durham. *Exodus*. Word Biblical Commentary. Volume 3. Waco, Texas: Word Books, Publisher, 1987.

H. L. Ellison. *Exodus*. The Daily Study Bible: Old Testament. Philadelphia: The Westminster Press, 1982.

Terence Fretheim. *Exodus*. Interpretation: A Bible Commentary for Teaching and Preaching. Louisville, Kentucky: John Knox Press, 1991.

Roy L. Honeycutt, Jr. "Exodus." *The Broadman Bible Commentary*. Volume 1. Nashville, Tennessee: Broadman Press, 1969.

Page H. Kelley. *Exodus: Called for Redemptive Mission*. Nashville, Tennessee: Convention Press, 1977.

Page H. Kelley. *Journey to the Land of Promise: Genesis—Deuteronomy*. Macon, Georgia: Smyth & Helwys Publishing, Inc., 1997.

The fourth unit, "Called to Worship Only God," considers passages from Exodus 25 through the end of the book. The emphasis of this portion of Exodus is on worship. The first lesson, from Exodus 32, focuses on worship gone astray. It is the story of the Israelites' breaking the covenant that they had only shortly before promised to keep. It is also the story that shows the greatness of Moses, who interceded with God not to destroy the people. In the second lesson, from Exodus 34, God renewed the covenant with the Israelites, giving them what is called the "ritual decalogue" to distinguish it from the "moral decalogue" of Exodus 20. The third lesson considers a subject that fills thirteen chapters in Exodus—chapters 25 through 31 and chapters 35 through 40. These chapters deal with building and furnishing the tabernacle, along with instructions about the priests who were to minister there. The sheer amount of space that is given to these instructions about the tabernacle clearly suggests that the tabernacle represented something important. Indeed it did, and the final lesson in the study will focus on the *why* of the tabernacle. The tabernacle spoke to the yearning of the Israelites to know that God was present with them. Thus, this lesson will speak to our own deep yearning to know that we are not alone but that God is with us.

UNIT ONE, PREPARATION FOR DELIVERANCE

Lesson 1	Just When Things Were Going So . . .	Exodus 1:6–10; 1:22—2:15; 2:23–25
Lesson 2	Excuses, Excuses	Exodus 3:1–14; 4:1–15

UNIT TWO, GOD'S POWER TO DELIVER

Lesson 3	The Futility of Resisting God	Exodus 7:1–6, 14–18; 8:1–3, 16,20–21; 9:1–4, 8–9, 22–26; 10:3–6, 21–23, 27–29
Lesson 4	A Night Never to Be Forgotten	Exodus 11:1–8; 12:21–32
Lesson 5	Sing to the Lord for Freedom!	Exodus 14:21—15:2, 20–21
Lesson 6	No Longer but Not Yet	Exodus 15:22—16:7; 17:1–7

UNIT THREE, GUIDANCE FOR COVENANT LIVING

Lesson 7   Wonderful Offer, Serious Demand   Exodus 19:1–12
Lesson 8   Treat God Like This   Exodus 20:1–11
Lesson 9   Treat People Like This   Exodus 20:12–17
Lesson 10   The Nitty-Gritty of Covenant Living   Exodus 21:12–17,
22–27; 22:21—23:11

UNIT FOUR, CALLED TO WORSHIP ONLY GOD

Lesson 11   A Broken Covenant
            and a Second Chance   Exodus 32:7–34
Lesson 12   Starting Over   Exodus 34:1–28
Lesson 13   God Dwelling Among Us   Exodus 25:1–8;
29:43–46; 33:7–11,
14–16; 40:16–38

NOTES

1. Page H. Kelley, *Exodus: Called for Redemptive Mission* (Nashville, Tennessee: Convention Press, 1977), 5.

2. Page H. Kelley, *Exodus: Called for Redemptive Mission* (Nashville, Tennessee: Convention Press, 1977), 5. See references to the Exodus event in Deuteronomy 6:20–25; 26:5–9; Joshua 24:1–7; Hosea 11:1; Amos 3:1–2; Micah 6:3–5; Psalm 77:11–20; 78; 105:26–45; 106; 114; 135; 136.

3. Unless otherwise indicated, all Scripture quotations in this study introduction are from the New Revised Standard Version.

4. Listing a book does not imply full agreement by the writers or BAPTISTWAY PRESS® with all of its comments.

Preparation for Deliverance

The second book of the Bible was not always known by the title "Exodus." Like the other books of the Pentateuch (the first five books of the Old Testament), it was originally known by the opening words of the book: *And these are the names*. However, the book later came to be known as "Exodus" because the central event around which the book develops is Israel's Exodus from Egypt.

Why is Israel's Exodus from Egypt so crucial? The rest of the Old Testament answers that question, but here are three reasons. For one thing, the Exodus was crucial because it shows the redemptive activity of God on behalf of God's people. In addition, this event anchors God's self-revelation in history. Further, this event becomes the basis for a covenant relationship between God and God's people.

Thus, the Book of Exodus revolves around the crucial event in Hebrew history. The Book of Exodus is also important because it links the activities described in Genesis that centered around Abraham, Isaac, Jacob, and Joseph, with the activities described in the remainder of the Old Testament that centered around the kings and the prophets.

Exodus then is the pivotal book of the Old Testament. Moreover, the pivotal event in the book was God's deliverance of the Hebrews from their Egyptian slavery.[1]

UNIT ONE, PREPARATION FOR DELIVERANCE

Lesson 1   Just When Things Were Going So . . .   Exodus 1:6–10;
                                                    1:22—2:15;
                                                    2:23–25
Lesson 2   Excuses, Excuses   Exodus 3:1–14;
                                                    4:1–15

NOTES

1. Unless otherwise indicated, all Scripture quotations in this unit of study are from the New International Version.

Focal Text

Exodus 1:6–10;
1:22—2:15; 2:23–25

Background

Exodus 1—2

Main Idea

God's providential care takes precedence over human evaluations, plans, and difficulties.

Question to Explore

Where is God in the mountain peaks, plateaus, and valleys of our lives?

Study Aim

To identify ways in which our human evaluations and plans need to be countered by the promise of God's providential care

Study and Action Emphases

- Affirm the Bible as our authoritative guide for life and ministry
- Share the gospel with all people
- Develop a growing, vibrant faith
- Include all God's family in decision-making and service
- Value all people as created in the image of God
- Encourage healthy families

LESSON ONE

Just When Things Were Going So . . .

Quick Read

Even as the Hebrews chafed under their brutal persecution as slaves to Pharaoh, God was preparing a deliverer for his people.

When I had been pastor of my first church for a year, I thought I was ready to move on to a larger assignment. So when the pastor search committee came from a larger church in Killeen, Texas, I was excited about the possibility. I thought I preached effectively, and the committee seemed to enjoy the service. So I was hopeful. I never heard from the pastor search committee again, however. At that juncture in my pastoral ministry, I was deeply hurt by this blatant rejection and wondered where God was in this process. A few months later, a pastor search committee came from a church in Waco, Texas. That church ultimately called me to be their pastor, and I discovered where God had been in the earlier process. God had been closing the door to that opportunity in Killeen that would have taken me another hour's drive away from Baylor University, where I was working on my Ph. D., so that God could get me to the church in Waco, where Baylor University is located.

At times God is so obviously at work in our lives that we cannot miss his presence. At other times, we have to dust for fingerprints to see whether God is there at all. In either case, God is at work, preparing us. What is true of God's children today was also true of God's children in Egypt during the time of their Egyptian slavery. Perhaps they too wondered where God was in the process. With the rise of Moses, they would discover where God was involved. God was preparing the deliverer for his people.

Exodus 1:6–10; 1:22—2:15

⁶Now Joseph and all his brothers and all that generation died, ⁷but the Israelites were fruitful and multiplied greatly and became exceedingly numerous, so that the land was filled with them.

⁸Then a new king, who did not know about Joseph, came to power in Egypt. ⁹"Look," he said to his people, "the Israelites have become much too numerous for us. ¹⁰Come, we must deal shrewdly with them or they will become even more numerous and, if war breaks out, will join our enemies, fight against us and leave the country."

. . . .

²²Then Pharaoh gave this order to all his people: "Every boy that is born you must throw into the Nile, but let every girl live."

²:¹Now a man of the house of Levi married a Levite woman, ²and she became pregnant and gave birth to a son. When she saw that he was a fine child, she hid him for three months. ³But when she could hide him

no longer, she got a papyrus basket for him and coated it with tar and pitch. Then she placed the child in it and put it among the reeds along the bank of the Nile. ⁴His sister stood at a distance to see what would happen to him.

⁵Then Pharaoh's daughter went down to the Nile to bathe, and her attendants were walking along the river bank. She saw the basket among the reeds and sent her slave girl to get it. ⁶She opened it and saw the baby. He was crying, and she felt sorry for him. "This is one of the Hebrew babies," she said.

⁷Then his sister asked Pharaoh's daughter, "Shall I go and get one of the Hebrew women to nurse the baby for you?"

⁸"Yes, go," she answered. And the girl went and got the baby's mother. ⁹Pharaoh's daughter said to her, "Take this baby and nurse him for me, and I will pay you." So the woman took the baby and nursed him. ¹⁰When the child grew older, she took him to Pharaoh's daughter and he became her son. She named him Moses, saying, "I drew him out of the water."

¹¹One day, after Moses had grown up, he went out to where his own people were and watched them at their hard labor. He saw an Egyptian beating a Hebrew, one of his own people. ¹²Glancing this way and that and seeing no one, he killed the Egyptian and hid him in the sand. ¹³The next day he went out and saw two Hebrews fighting. He asked the one in the wrong, "Why are you hitting your fellow Hebrew?"

¹⁴The man said, "Who made you ruler and judge over us? Are you thinking of killing me as you killed the Egyptian?" Then Moses was afraid and thought, "What I did must have become known."

¹⁵When Pharaoh heard of this, he tried to kill Moses, but Moses fled from Pharaoh and went to live in Midian, where he sat down by a well.

Exodus 2:23–25

²³During that long period, the king of Egypt died. The Israelites groaned in their slavery and cried out, and their cry for help because of their slavery went up to God. ²⁴God heard their groaning and he remembered his covenant with Abraham, with Isaac and with Jacob. ²⁵So God looked on the Israelites and was concerned about them.

Background of the Biblical Story

The first seven verses of Exodus connect the story told in Exodus with the stories already told in Genesis, stories of individuals who were chosen by

God to fulfill God's plan for the redemption of the world and who were fortified by God's promises. These promises were given first to Abraham (Genesis 12:1–3), then to Isaac (Gen. 26:3–4), and later to Jacob (28:13–15). These promises were now being fulfilled in Jacob's sons.

In the list in Exodus 1:1–4, the sons of Jacob's wives, Leah and Rachel (Reuben through Benjamin), are placed in order of their seniority ahead of the sons of his two concubines (Dan through Asher). Joseph is listed separately since he was already in Egypt. Through these sons of Jacob, God would fulfill the promises originally given to Abraham.

How did the Hebrews get to Egypt in the first place? The answer to that question is found in the story of Joseph. As the favored son of Jacob, Joseph incurred the wrath of his brothers, who sold him as a slave to a band of Midianites. They took Joseph to Egypt. There he ended up a slave in the household of Potiphar, one of the primary assistants to the Pharaoh. Because of his unique gifts, Joseph was called on to interpret the dreams of Pharaoh. He was then placed in charge of preparing for the years of famine revealed through Pharaoh's dreams. Eventually, when the effects of the famine reached into the land known as Canaan, Jacob sent his sons to Egypt to obtain some food. They were ushered into the presence of their long lost brother, Joseph. Joseph forgave his brothers, was reconciled with his family, and brought all of his family, including his father Jacob, to Egypt, where he could care for them. With the death of Joseph and the passing of years, attitudes changed toward these Hebrews, as we shall see in this week's lesson.

> *At times God is so obviously at work in our lives that we cannot miss his presence. At other times, we have to dust for fingerprints to see whether God is there at all.*

Pharaoh's Fear (1:6–8)

The biblical writers were historians, but they were selective historians. Instead of giving a strict chronological account of events, they focused on certain events crucial to their purpose and omitted details that did not contribute to their purpose. Consequently, we often notice lapses of time in the biblical narrative. Such a lapse is apparent in verses 6 and 8. The whole generation of people identified in verses 1–4 had passed from the scene. Even Joseph had been forgotten. Between verses 5 and 6 stand decades, perhaps even centuries. That is why the Egyptian leader introduced in verse 8 did not know who Joseph was or why this large contingency of Hebrew slaves were in Egypt.

Who was this pharaoh introduced in verse 8? Scholars have gravitated between two answers to that question, based on their dating of the Exodus of the Hebrew slaves from Egypt under Moses' leadership. Some have dated the Exodus in the middle of the fifteenth century B.C., about 1450. Others have dated the Exodus in the thirteenth century B.C., around 1250. To me, the evidence points to the thirteenth-century date for the Exodus. If this is correct, then the pharaoh in our story could be Sethos I, who ruled over Egypt about 1309–1290 B.C., and the pharaoh of the Exodus could be Rameses II, who ruled about 1290–1224 B.C. Precise identification of the pharaohs of the oppression and the Exodus is uncertain, however.

Through this joint Hebrew and Egyptian heritage, God prepared Moses for his role as deliverer.

How contemporary the story seems as we see how Pharaoh's fear of losing his power and his possessions drove him into oppressive treatment of the Hebrews. Change the names and the location, and this story could be the headline of today's newspaper. National leaders who instigate genocide and CEOs who oppress their employees are simply modern versions of the Egyptian leader in our story.

Bring it down to the personal level, and we see examples of the same kind of behavior. Driven by the fear of losing what we have, many push aside both ethical standards and rules of propriety. The pharaoh of Egypt clearly demonstrates that abuse of power.

Pharaoh's Strategies (1:22)

Pharaoh's initial strategy to minimize the threat of these Hebrews living in his land was forced labor. Cruel taskmasters would exact from the Hebrew slaves every ounce of strength in their bodies to build great cities to honor the Pharaoh and provide storage for his bounty. But the harder the Egyptians pushed the Hebrew slaves, the stronger the Hebrews grew. Instead of decreasing the strength of the Hebrews, the oppression and ruthlessness of the Egyptian taskmasters created the soil for their continued growth (1:11–14).

When the strategy of enforced labor failed, the Pharaoh adopted a more sinister strategy. He ordered the Hebrew midwives to kill every male baby born to Hebrew women. Only the female babies could be spared. It was not uncommon in the ancient world for female babies to be discarded and male babies to be valued highly. However, the Pharaoh reversed the process. Without male Hebrews, he thought, the Hebrew population would eventually die out. However, the midwives refused to follow Pharaoh's orders, devising an ingenuous excuse to avoid punishment (1:19). Pharaoh simply intensified his strategy by ordering all Hebrews to cast their male babies into the Nile River, where they would drown.

> God is still at work today, calling individuals to special service in his kingdom.

Already, God's promises to Abraham were being fulfilled. God promised to make of Abraham and his descendants a numerous people (Gen. 15:5). He also promised Abraham that his descendants would be oppressed in a strange land (15:13). Even in the midst of their oppression, then, God was at work carrying out his promises.

The Rise of Moses (2:1–10)

God would carry out his promises through a special leader named Moses. Chapter 1 ends with a description of the persecution of the Hebrews. Chapter 2 begins with a description of the preparation of the deliverer for the Hebrew people. The biblical writer reveals the amazing preparation

The Name *Moses*

When Pharaoh's daughter decided to adopt the Hebrew baby she discovered floating in the Nile, she named him Moses. Where did the name come from? Scholars take one of two positions.

Some, based on the implication of Exodus 2:10, suggest that the name came from the Hebrew words *mo* and *ushe*, which mean *to draw out*, because she "drew him out of the water." Since she knew the baby was a Hebrew child, giving the child a Hebrew name would not be unusual.

On the other hand, some scholars are not convinced that the daughter of the Pharaoh of Egypt would give her son a Hebrew name. They trace the name instead to an Egyptian word *mes* or *mesu* or *meses* that connotes *to give birth*. This Egyptian word means *born of* or *son of*. So Ra-meses was the son of Ra, and Tutmoses was the son of Tut. The name *Moses* thus was the shortened form of a once longer Egyptian word.

of Moses for the task to which God called him. In our text for this week's lesson, we see two dimensions of this preparation: Moses' preparation as a Hebrew and his preparation as an Egyptian prince.

We see first of all Moses' connection with the people he was to deliver. He was of the house of Levi (2:1). When he was born, his mother did not want to discard him as the Pharaoh had instructed. However, after three months, she knew she could no longer keep his presence secret. So she did as the Pharaoh had instructed (1:22). She put her baby in the Nile River. She mitigated that action in three ways, however. She placed him in a basket that would float; she placed the basket near the shoreline; and she assigned her daughter to guard the basket.

We also see Moses' connection with those who oppressed the Hebrews. While Pharaoh's daughter bathed in the Nile, she saw Moses floating in the basket (2:5). She recognized immediately that this was a Hebrew baby. What would she do? Would she simply leave the baby there to die? Surely she was aware of Pharaoh's orders concerning these male Hebrew babies. In her moment of hesitation, Moses' sister took the initiative. She presumed that the Pharaoh's daughter would keep the baby and offered to find someone to nurse the baby for her.

Why would Pharaoh's daughter keep this Hebrew baby? One suggestion plays on the tradition that attributes fertility-inducing power to the water of the Nile River. Perhaps Pharaoh's daughter had not been able to have a child, and so she bathed in the Nile, hoping that the water would impart fruitfulness. In that frame of mind, she might have concluded that this baby was a gift from the gods. That is simply one suggestion. The Bible does not explain why Pharaoh's daughter kept this Hebrew baby. However, the Bible makes clear that because of his adoption by the Pharaoh's daughter, Moses was exposed to the wisdom of Egypt. In Stephen's sermon to the Sanhedrin, Stephen affirmed that Pharaoh's daughter took Moses and brought him up as her own son and that consequently Moses was educated in all the wisdom of the Egyptians (Acts 7:21–22).

. . . God prepares us for what God is preparing for us.

At the same time, Moses was nurtured in the traditions of the Hebrew people because his mother was his nursemaid (Exod. 2:9–10). During those early years of his life, Moses' mother taught him the stories of his ancestors, beginning with Abraham and going all the way through Joseph, who himself had held a position of authority in Egypt. Moses was therefore familiar with all the promises God made to the Hebrews and all the adventures of his ancestors. Moses was part and parcel of the Hebrew heritage. Through this joint Hebrew and Egyptian heritage, God prepared Moses for his role as deliverer.

The Fall of Moses (2:11–15)

Moses' training was not yet complete. God would also prepare him as a wilderness shepherd (2:16—3:1). The incident that triggered Moses' exile into the wilderness marks the beginning of his transition from Egyptian prince to deliverer. Again, the Bible is selective in the information it provides for us concerning Moses. How many details the biblical writer omitted between, "Take this baby and nurse him for me" in verse 9, and, "When the child grew older" in verse 10, and "One day, after Moses had grown up," in verse 11. Forty years of Moses' life are summarized in those three succinct phrases. This selectiveness is intentional. The biblical writer tells us what is needed to accomplish the purpose. During those years, Moses apparently struggled with an increasing tension between his biological heritage as a Hebrew and his adopted heritage as a member of Pharaoh's family. The biblical writer selected one incident within that time frame that clearly demonstrates this tension.

God's people still have to make choices today in response to God's calling.

The implication of verse 11 is that Moses was isolated from the Hebrews during his early years. Isolated in the royal household, he was not aware of the miserable conditions prevailing among his Hebrew brothers. When he saw an Egyptian beating a Hebrew slave, he came to the aid of the slave, killing the Egyptian in the process. His attempts to cover up his intervention were unsuccessful. Word eventually came to Pharaoh. He was enraged. Consequently, Moses had to flee for his life. At first glance, this turn of events seemed to undermine God's plan for Moses' life. In reality, Moses' escape from Pharaoh's rage was part of God's plan, for Moses was not yet ready to be God's deliverer. He still needed to be schooled in the university of the wilderness. To accomplish that final part of his training, God had to remove him from the influence of the royal household of Egypt.

Moses' intervention on behalf of his oppressed Hebrew brother was a deliberate choice to identify with his Hebrew heritage instead of his

Responding

The Apostle Paul presents an excellent case study of how to respond to the unpleasant experiences of our lives. As he pursued his calling, Paul was arrested and eventually thrown into prison in Rome. However, when he wrote to the Philippians about his prison experience, he did not complain. Instead, he was thankful for his experience because his prison stay enabled him to share the gospel with the elite members of the Roman guard, something that never would have happened apart from his imprisonment (Philippians 1:12–14). What experiences in your life, that at first glance you consider hindrances, may instead be God's opportunities?

Egyptian heritage, according to Hebrews 11:24–25. Too, his intervention on behalf of the Hebrew slave reflects characteristics that would later appear in a more mature form in his life. For one thing, Moses was willing to identify with his people. In addition, he had a passionate desire for justice. Further, he was willing to thrust himself into a difficult situation as a mediator. When Moses later returned to confront Pharaoh on behalf of his people and carry out the purpose of God, these emerging qualities would come to full bloom.

God opens doors of opportunity for us, but we have to move through them.

God's Continuing Concern (2:23–25)

Even if we did not know the story of Moses, we might suspect that something important was about to happen. Exodus 2:23–25 provides further evidence for that belief. In the depth of their oppression, the Israelites "groaned" and "cried out" to God for help. Note the four verbs in 2:24–25 that describe God's actions: "God heard"; "he remembered"; "God looked on"; "God was concerned."

At many points in Exodus 1—2, we can see reversals and contrasts. Just when the Pharaoh thought he had the Hebrews under subjection, the Israelites grew in number. The mighty Pharaoh found himself thwarted by two Hebrew midwives. Then, when the Pharaoh sought to kill all the Hebrew baby boys, the Pharaoh's own daughter thwarted his efforts.

Exodus 2:23–25 depicts the contrast between the Israelites' deep need and God's concern and awareness. Just when things looked so bad for the

Hebrews and all hope seemed gone, something was about to happen. God was about to intervene on their behalf.

Implications for Today

God is still at work today, calling individuals to special service in his kingdom. Whom God calls, God prepares. Sometimes God prepares us by placing certain people in our lives. Sometimes God prepares us by opening doors of opportunity for us. Sometimes God prepares us by closing doors. In all of these ways, and in many other ways, God prepares us for what God is preparing for us.

God's people still have to make choices today in response to God's calling. God called Moses to a unique ministry, and God prepared Moses in extraordinary ways. Yet Moses had to choose God's calling, and he had to incorporate God's preparation. Ultimately, Moses had to move through the doors of opportunity God opened before him. The same thing is true of us today. God opens doors of opportunity for us, but we have to move through them.

QUESTIONS

1. What is God calling you to do in his kingdom today?

2. What are some ways in which God has prepared you for that calling?

3. Can you think of a time when God was at work in your life but you were only able to discern his work from a later perspective?

4. What choices are facing you as you implement God's calling for your life?

Focal Text

Exodus 3:1–14; 4:1–15

Background

Exodus 3—4

Main Idea

Our reasons for resisting God's call are really only excuses.

Question to Explore

What are your favorite excuses for resisting God's call?

Study Aim

To compare the futility of Moses' excuses to my own excuses for resisting God's call

Study and Action Emphases

- Affirm the Bible as our authoritative guide for life and ministry
- Share the gospel with all people
- Develop a growing, vibrant faith
- Include all God's family in decision-making and service
- Value all people as created in the image of God
- Equip people for servant leadership

LESSON TWO

Excuses, Excuses

Quick Read

Even though Moses felt inadequate for the task, he eventually responded positively to the call to become God's deliverer for the Hebrews in Egyptian captivity.

As a young pastor, serving at the First Baptist Church of Calvert, Texas, I wanted to make a difference in the lives of the young people of our town. So I planned a number of events that would draw in the Calvert youth who were not directly connected to our church. For example, one young woman attended our youth camp that first summer. Her father was known throughout the community as an alcoholic. Her mother suffered from an illness that also limited her effectiveness as a parent. So this teenager was adrift, not certain who she was or what God wanted her to do with her life.

That week, however, God did something special in her life. Before the week was over, she had committed her life to Christ. I asked her to share her testimony in the morning worship service just a couple of weeks later. She was terrified at the thought of standing before all of the "respectable" people of the community. Yet, because of her new passion for God, she was willing to give it a try. Seated behind her on that Sunday morning, I could see her knees shaking as she moved to the pulpit to share her testimony.

Her testimony was succinct but profound. "I was a nobody," she told the congregation that morning, "but God has made me a somebody." No one in attendance that day ever forgot the impact of her testimony. Her availability to God allowed God to speak through her in an effective way.

Even though Moses initially balked when God called him to deliver the Hebrews from slavery, he eventually discovered that God could use him if he would make himself available.

Exodus 3:1–14

[1]Now Moses was tending the flock of Jethro his father-in-law, the priest of Midian, and he led the flock to the far side of the desert and came to Horeb, the mountain of God. [2]There the angel of the LORD appeared to him in flames of fire from within a bush. Moses saw that though the bush was on fire it did not burn up. [3]So Moses thought, "I will go over and see this strange sight—why the bush does not burn up."

[4]When the LORD saw that he had gone over to look, God called to him from within the bush, "Moses! Moses!"

And Moses said, "Here I am."

[5]"Do not come any closer," God said. "Take off your sandals, for the place where you are standing is holy ground." [6]Then he said, "I am the God of your father, the God of Abraham, the God of Isaac and the God of Jacob." At this, Moses hid his face, because he was afraid to look at God.

[7]The LORD said, "I have indeed seen the misery of my people in Egypt. I have heard them crying out because of their slave drivers, and I am concerned about their suffering. [8]So I have come down to rescue them from the hand of the Egyptians and to bring them up out of that land into a good and spacious land, a land flowing with milk and honey—the home of the Canaanites, Hittites, Amorites, Perizzites, Hivites and Jebusites. [9]And now the cry of the Israelites has reached me, and I have seen the way the Egyptians are oppressing them. [10]So now, go. I am sending you to Pharaoh to bring my people the Israelites out of Egypt."

[11]But Moses said to God, "Who am I, that I should go to Pharaoh and bring the Israelites out of Egypt?"

[12]And God said, "I will be with you. And this will be the sign to you that it is I who have sent you: When you have brought the people out of Egypt, you will worship God on this mountain."

[13]Moses said to God, "Suppose I go to the Israelites and say to them, 'The God of your fathers has sent me to you,' and they ask me, 'What is his name?' Then what shall I tell them?"

[14]God said to Moses, "I AM WHO I AM. This is what you are to say to the Israelites: 'I AM has sent me to you.'"

Exodus 4:1–15

[1]Moses answered, "What if they do not believe me or listen to me and say, 'The LORD did not appear to you'?"

[2]Then the LORD said to him, "What is that in your hand?"

"A staff," he replied.

[3]The LORD said, "Throw it on the ground."

Moses threw it on the ground and it became a snake, and he ran from it. [4]Then the LORD said to him, "Reach out your hand and take it by the tail." So Moses reached out and took hold of the snake and it turned back into a staff in his hand. [5]"This," said the LORD, "is so that they may believe that the LORD, the God of their fathers—the God of Abraham, the God of Isaac and the God of Jacob—has appeared to you."

[6]Then the LORD said, "Put your hand inside your cloak." So Moses put his hand into his cloak, and when he took it out, it was leprous, like snow.

[7]"Now put it back into your cloak," he said. So Moses put his hand back into his cloak, and when he took it out, it was restored, like the rest of his flesh.

[8]Then the LORD said, "If they do not believe you or pay attention to the first miraculous sign, they may believe the second. [9]But if they do not believe these two signs or listen to you, take some water from the Nile

and pour it on the dry ground. The water you take from the river will become blood on the ground."

[10]Moses said to the LORD, "O Lord, I have never been eloquent, neither in the past nor since you have spoken to your servant. I am slow of speech and tongue."

[11]The LORD said to him, "Who gave man his mouth? Who makes him deaf or mute? Who gives him sight or makes him blind? Is it not I, the LORD? [12]Now go; I will help you speak and will teach you what to say."

[13]But Moses said, "O Lord, please send someone else to do it."

[14]Then the LORD's anger burned against Moses and he said, "What about your brother, Aaron the Levite? I know he can speak well. He is already on his way to meet you, and his heart will be glad when he sees you. [15]You shall speak to him and put words in his mouth; I will help both of you speak and will teach you what to do.

Background of the Biblical Story

In a few bold strokes, the Bible portrays the ascent of Moses from slave boy to royal prince in Egypt (Exodus 2:8–10). From his biological mother, who was called in as his nursemaid, Moses was exposed to the rich heritage of the Hebrew people. From his adopted mother, who was the daughter of the Pharaoh, he was exposed to "all the wisdom of the Egyptians" (Acts 7:22). In just fifteen verses (Exod. 2:1–15), the Bible summarizes the first forty years of Moses' life (see Acts 7:23). At that point, Moses was expelled abruptly from his privileged life because he had come to the defense of a fellow Hebrew and had killed the guard who was abusing this servant.

"I was a nobody . . . but God has made me a somebody."

Moses escaped to Midian, where God would continue Moses' training. Midian stretched east and southward from the Jordan River and the Dead Sea, including most of the Sinai Peninsula. When Moses escaped from Egypt, he connected with a certain Midianite named Jethro, whose daughter, Zipporah, Moses later married (Exod. 2:15–21).

Again, we see the historical selectivity of the biblical writer, for the Scriptures once more cover vast periods of time in brief sentences. The biblical writer moved from Moses' first encounter with Zipporah (2:16), to their marriage (2:22), to the birth of their first son (2:23), covering a period of several months and perhaps even years in two sentences.

According to Stephen in his later sermon recorded in Acts, forty more years passed between Moses' flight from Egypt and his encounter with God at the burning bush, a period of time covered by the biblical writer in eleven verses (Acts 7:30).

Purposefully, the Bible focuses on the key events in God's unfolding purpose. Therefore, when coming to such a significant event as the burning bush experience, the biblical writer slowed to a snail's pace and gave nearly two chapters to this single event.

God's Call (3:1–10)

Why did the biblical writer spend so much time describing the burning bush experience? The answer is simple. At the burning bush Moses had an encounter with the living God who gave him the calling for his life.

The place of the encounter is Horeb, identified by the biblical writer as "the mountain of God" (3:1). The location is also called Mount Sinai. Sinai and Horeb refer to the same place (see 19:1–2; Deuteronomy 5:2). This was called "the mountain of God" because of its significance in Hebrew history. Here God gave his law to Israel and established his covenant with his chosen people (Exod. 19—24).

> *Purposefully, the Bible focuses on the key events in God's unfolding purpose.*

"The Angel of the Lord"

Although Moses' encounter at the burning bush was obviously with God himself, the story begins with the announcement that "the angel of the Lord appeared to him in flames of fire from within a bush" (Exodus 3:2). Was it "the angel of the Lord" or the Lord himself whom Moses encountered in the wilderness? In some Old Testament references, the angel of the Lord seems to be different from God. For example, in Exodus 23:20–23, God promised Moses that he was sending his angel ahead of them to guard them as they moved into the Promised Land. Yet in other instances, the angel of the Lord seems to be identical with God, and the two seem to be interchangeable. For example, in Genesis 16:7–13, when Abraham sent Hagar away, the angel of the Lord came to Hagar in the wilderness with promises of God's blessings and protection. But then, when Hagar responded in gratitude, she said to the angel of the Lord, "You are the God who sees me" (Genesis 16:13). In Moses' burning bush encounter, the angel of the Lord represents a visible presence of God himself.

Here, discouraged and fearful, the prophet Elijah was renewed by God's presence (1 Kings 19:4–8). Here, too, at this sacred spot, Moses had his first encounter with the covenant God of Israel.

What drew Moses to the burning bush to begin with, however, was not commitment but curiosity. He observed that the bush was on fire but the fire did not consume it. He moved closer to satisfy his curiosity. As he did, he received his calling.

The opening phrase in verse 4—"When the Lord saw that he had gone over to look, God called to him from within the bush"—is intriguing. The verse suggests that God was ready to issue his call to Moses, but Moses had to make an initial response. Had Moses not gone over to look, would God have issued his call in some other way? Or would God have turned to someone else to be Israel's deliverer?

Moses' curiosity was soon eclipsed by awe as he recognized the holiness of this place and the majesty of the One speaking to him from the burning bush. The One speaking to Moses was none other than the covenant God of Israel, who had earlier spoken to Abraham and Isaac and Jacob.

With brutal honesty, the Bible reflects Moses' hesitancy to accept such a calling and his feeling of unworthiness for such a task.

What this recognition triggered in Moses we can only guess. Surely the stories of God's promises to his ancestors that he had learned from his mother exploded into his consciousness. What did this God want with Moses? Moses did not have to wait long to find out.

The oppression of the Hebrew slaves that had provoked action on Moses' part earlier would now provoke God to action (compare Exod. 3:7 and 2:24). God had heard the cry of his people; God was touched by their need; and God had decided to deliver them.

Two elements of this deliverance become clear in God's communication to Moses. First, this deliverance would fulfill the promises given earlier to Abraham, for God would establish the released captives in the land God had promised to Abraham. Perhaps God's reference to "the Canaanites, Hittites, Amorites, Perizzites, Hivites and Jebusites" was simply an acknowledgement of the spaciousness of the land (3:8). The land in which God would establish Israel was big enough to hold six nations. It would surely be adequate for the one nation of Israel.

The other element of God's communication to Moses was the startling announcement that God had chosen Moses to be Israel's deliverer. God called Moses by name and explained to Moses that he was to go to Egypt and confront Pharaoh. Further, Moses was to convince Pharaoh to release the Hebrew slaves. He was to then lead the released slaves to the land God promised to give them. Moses was to be the instrument through whom the promises to Abraham would be fulfilled.

How would Moses respond to such a revelation? With brutal honesty, the Bible reflects Moses' hesitancy to accept such a calling and his feeling of unworthiness for such a task. As most of us would have responded in that situation—in fact, as most of us respond to God's calling in our lives today—Moses responded with excuses. To each excuse God gave a clarifying response.

Moses' Excuses (3:11–14; 4:1–15)

Moses' initial excuse, as for us on most occasions, was a lack of self-confidence. "Who am I," Moses protested (3:11), *that I should be Israel's deliverer?* His assertion, *I can't do this,* reflected a misunderstanding of how God accomplishes his work. God works through individuals like Moses—and like you and me—but the success of God's ventures does not depend on our adequacy but on the adequacy of God. God corrected Moses' misunderstanding by reminding Moses that he would be with him to guarantee his success (3:12).

> *As most of us would have responded in that situation—in fact, as most of us respond to God's calling in our lives today—Moses responded with excuses.*

With his attention now properly focused on God, Moses introduced a second excuse. He could not go unless he knew God's name (3:13). Moses' desire to know God's name was driven by two understandings of that day. On the one hand, to know the name of a god was to acknowledge a special intimacy with that god. Thus, to know God's name was to know God. In addition, to speak the name of one's god was to identify the god's attributes and character. So Moses' desire to know God's name fit into the popular beliefs of the day. Perhaps knowing the name of God was important to Moses for another reason. His fellow Hebrews, after the passing of many years, might have begun to worship the many gods of Egypt. To call them to a new allegiance, Moses would have to present to them in a specific and articulate way this God whom he had encountered in the burning bush. So, Moses wanted to know God's name.

Moses' Experience and Yours

In studying this lesson, recognize that what Moses experienced we can also experience today:

- God continues to reveal himself to those who are able and willing to see.
- God continues to call ordinary individuals to carry out extraordinary assignments.
- The successful fulfillment of these assignments still does not depend on our ability but on our availability.

God identified himself as "I AM" (3:14). What did God mean by that name? His response could have been a reflection of his *mystery.* He may have been saying, *The nature of God cannot be expressed in a name. You will see who I am by what I do.* Or, God's response could have been a reflection of his *adequacy.* He may have been saying, *I am all that I need to be to carry out my plans.* Or, God's response could have been a reflection of his *creativity.* He may have been say-

... God often makes himself known in surprising ways and at unexpected times.

ing, *I will bring about what I will bring about.* Whichever of those ideas was primary, God went on to identify himself with "the God of your fathers" (3:15). In other words, this mysterious, adequate, creative God encountering Moses in the burning bush was the same God who had issued his covenant promises to Abraham and Isaac and Jacob. Now God was ready to bring to reality those promises God had made to them.

Surprisingly, Moses was not yet done with his excuse making. *How can I make them believe me?* That was Moses' next excuse (4:1). God provided three signs of authority for Moses: the rod that turned into a serpent (4:2–5); the hand that became leprous (4:6–8); and the water that turned into blood (4:9). These miraculous actions by Moses would be signs that pointed beyond themselves to the one who performed them, but even more, beyond the one who performed them to the God who had sent him. It was not belief in Moses but belief in the God of Moses that ultimately inspired the people.

Even after God provided these signs to Moses, Moses was still not convinced. Perhaps he remembered the eloquence of the Pharaoh. Maybe he feared that after forty years of absence from the Egyptian court, his rhetorical skills had atrophied. Or perhaps, as verse 13 implies, Moses just didn't want to go back to Egypt. God's patience was wearing thin. Yet, even as God reminded Moses again that the adequacy was not in Moses but in God, God assigned Aaron, who was more articulate in his speech, to accompany Moses in carrying out the assignment.

The scene was now set. God had his leader. Moses was ready to face Pharaoh and deliver God's people.

Implications for Today

This experience in the life of Moses articulates a truth that runs throughout the Bible: God is a God who makes himself known. To Moses, God made himself known through the burning bush. To Jacob, God made himself known in a dream (Gen. 32). To Isaiah, God made himself known in the temple (Isaiah 6). To Paul, God made himself known in a dramatic epiphany (Acts 9). God is a God who makes himself known. So God does to us, breaking into our lives to reveal his nature and unfold before us his plan for our lives.

Further, God often makes himself known in surprising ways and at unexpected times. In the wilderness, Moses was far removed from any religious community. Neither was he on a religious pilgrimage that day in the wilderness. Instead, Moses was simply carrying out the mundane duties in an ordinary way. Yet in the commonplace ordinariness of Moses' activities, God revealed himself in an extraordinary way. So God does to us, revealing himself in unexpected ways and at unexpected times.

God uses imperfect individuals like Moses—and like you and me. . . .

This experience in the life of Moses also acknowledges another truth that runs throughout the Bible: God uses imperfect individuals like Moses—and like you and me—to carry out his kingdom work. Moses, who helped to shape our understanding of God, began with a faulty understanding of God. Moses, the great spokesperson for God's cause, was not able to speak well. Moses, who courageously confronted Pharaoh, was initially afraid to confront him. God chose to use a limited, marred human being to carry out a special assignment. So God does still today, using individuals with an inadequate understanding of him, with limited abilities, and with timid spirits to carry out God's kingdom work.

QUESTIONS

1. In what ways does God make his will known to people today?

2. If someone were to ask you to describe God, what would you say?

3. What inadequacies do you often allow to stand in the way of your service for God?

4. What resources has God made available to you as you have responded positively to his calling?

5. Who has God given you to assist you in fulfilling your calling?

God's Power to Deliver

Unit two, "God's Power to Deliver," begins with Moses' return to Egypt and confrontation of Pharaoh. When Pharaoh refused God's message, God began to send a series of plagues on Egypt. These miraculous actions demonstrated that God was more powerful than Pharaoh and the gods of Egypt. At last came the terrible night of the tenth plague, which was commemorated by the Hebrews in the institution of Passover. Shocked and grieved by the loss of firstborn people and livestock all across Egypt, Pharaoh at last agreed to let the Hebrews go.

Lesson three deals with the first nine plagues, and lesson four with the tenth. Lesson five is a study of God's deliverance of the Hebrews through the sea and their rejoicing afterward. Lesson six considers the Hebrews' grumbling in the wilderness and God's provision for them by sending manna, quail, and water. The background Scriptures for this unit are from Exodus 5—18.[1]

UNIT TWO, GOD'S POWER TO DELIVER

Lesson 3	The Futility of Resisting God	Exodus 7:1–6, 14–18; 8:1–3, 16, 20–21; 9:1–4, 8–9, 22–26; 10:3–6, 21–23, 27–29
Lesson 4	A Night Never to Be Forgotten	Exodus 11:1–8; 12:21–32
Lesson 5	Sing to the Lord for Freedom!	Exodus 14:21— 15:2, 20–21
Lesson 6	No Longer but Not Yet	Exodus 15:22— 16:7; 17:1–7

NOTES

1. Unless otherwise indicated, all Scripture quotations in this unit of study are from the New International Version.

Focal Text

Exodus 7:1–6, 14–18;
8:1–3, 16, 20–21;
9:1–4, 8–9, 22–26;
10:3–6, 21–23, 27–29

Background

Exodus 5—10

Main Idea

The greatness of God's power makes resistance to God's way futile.

Question to Explore

Why do human beings foolishly resist God and bring misery on themselves?

Study Aim

To describe the first nine plagues and summarize their meaning

Study and Action Emphases

- Affirm the Bible as our authoritative guide for life and ministry
- Share the gospel with all people
- Develop a growing, vibrant faith

LESSON THREE

The Futility of Resisting God

Quick Read

The battle was not between Moses and Pharaoh but between Moses' God and Pharaoh's gods. The cumulative effect of the nine plagues was to demonstrate the superior power of Yahweh.

The little girl interrupted her Sunday School teacher, who was telling the story of David and Goliath. The teacher had said, "David was brave to face Goliath." The little girl responded, "It was not David who was brave but Goliath." The teacher was puzzled and asked for an explanation. The little girl explained, "Goliath was the brave one because he had to go out alone. But David had God with him." Because we know that God is with us today, we too can face the forces of darkness unafraid.

Exodus 7:1–6, 14–18

[1] Then the LORD said to Moses, "See, I have made you like God to Pharaoh, and your brother Aaron will be your prophet. [2] You are to say everything I command you, and your brother Aaron is to tell Pharaoh to let the Israelites go out of his country. [3] But I will harden Pharaoh's heart, and though I multiply my miraculous signs and wonders in Egypt, [4] he will not listen to you. Then I will lay my hand on Egypt and with mighty acts of judgment I will bring out my divisions, my people the Israelites. [5] And the Egyptians will know that I am the LORD when I stretch out my hand against Egypt and bring the Israelites out of it."

[6] Moses and Aaron did just as the LORD commanded them.

. . . .

[14] Then the LORD said to Moses, "Pharaoh's heart is unyielding; he refuses to let the people go. [15] Go to Pharaoh in the morning as he goes out to the water. Wait on the bank of the Nile to meet him, and take in your hand the staff that was changed into a snake. [16] Then say to him, 'The LORD, the God of the Hebrews, has sent me to say to you: Let my people go, so that they may worship me in the desert. But until now you have not listened. [17] This is what the LORD says: By this you will know that I am the LORD: With the staff that is in my hand I will strike the water of the Nile, and it will be changed into blood. [18] The fish in the Nile will die, and the river will stink; the Egyptians will not be able to drink its water.'"

Exodus 8:1–3, 16, 20–21

[1] Then the LORD said to Moses, "Go to Pharaoh and say to him, 'This is what the LORD says: Let my people go, so that they may worship me. [2] If you refuse to let them go, I will plague your whole country with frogs. [3] The Nile will teem with frogs. They will come up into your palace and your bedroom and onto your bed, into the houses of your officials and on your people, and into your ovens and kneading troughs.

[16]Then the LORD said to Moses, "Tell Aaron, 'Stretch out your staff and strike the dust of the ground,' and throughout the land of Egypt the dust will become gnats."

[20]Then the LORD said to Moses, "Get up early in the morning and confront Pharaoh as he goes to the water and say to him, 'This is what the LORD says: Let my people go, so that they may worship me. [21]If you do not let my people go, I will send swarms of flies on you and your officials, on your people and into your houses. The houses of the Egyptians will be full of flies, and even the ground where they are.

Exodus 9:1–4, 8–9, 22–26

[1]Then the LORD said to Moses, "Go to Pharaoh and say to him, 'This is what the LORD, the God of the Hebrews, says: "Let my people go, so that they may worship me." [2]If you refuse to let them go and continue to hold them back, [3]the hand of the LORD will bring a terrible plague on your livestock in the field—on your horses and donkeys and camels and on your cattle and sheep and goats. [4]But the LORD will make a distinction between the livestock of Israel and that of Egypt, so that no animal belonging to the Israelites will die.'"

[8]Then the LORD said to Moses and Aaron, "Take handfuls of soot from a furnace and have Moses toss it into the air in the presence of Pharaoh. [9]It will become fine dust over the whole land of Egypt, and festering boils will break out on men and animals throughout the land."

[22]Then the LORD said to Moses, "Stretch out your hand toward the sky so that hail will fall all over Egypt—on men and animals and on everything growing in the fields of Egypt." [23]When Moses stretched out his staff toward the sky, the LORD sent thunder and hail, and lightning flashed down to the ground. So the LORD rained hail on the land of Egypt; [24]hail fell and lightning flashed back and forth. It was the worst storm in all the land of Egypt since it had become a nation. [25]Throughout Egypt hail struck everything in the fields—both men and animals; it beat down everything growing in the fields and stripped every tree. [26]The only place it did not hail was the land of Goshen, where the Israelites were.

Exodus 10:3–6, 21–23, 27–29

[3]So Moses and Aaron went to Pharaoh and said to him, "This is what the LORD, the God of the Hebrews, says: 'How long will you refuse to humble yourself before me? Let my people go, so that they may worship me. [4]If you refuse to let them go, I will bring locusts into your country tomorrow. [5]They will cover the face of the ground so that it cannot be seen. They will devour what little you have left after the hail, including every tree that is growing in your fields. [6]They will fill your houses and those of all your officials and all the Egyptians—something neither your fathers nor your forefathers have ever seen from the day they settled in this land till now.'" Then Moses turned and left Pharaoh.

. . . .

[21]Then the LORD said to Moses, "Stretch out your hand toward the sky so that darkness will spread over Egypt—darkness that can be felt." [22]So Moses stretched out his hand toward the sky, and total darkness covered all Egypt for three days. [23]No one could see anyone else or leave his place for three days. Yet all the Israelites had light in the places where they lived.

. . . .

[27]But the LORD hardened Pharaoh's heart, and he was not willing to let them go. [28]Pharaoh said to Moses, "Get out of my sight! Make sure you do not appear before me again! The day you see my face you will die."
[29]"Just as you say," Moses replied, "I will never appear before you again."

Background of the Biblical Story

As Moses returned to Egypt, the battle lines were set between the God of Israel and the gods of Egypt. The triumph of Yahweh is described in a skillfully told story of ten incidents, traditionally known as the Ten Plagues. Since "plague" is a disease in common parlance, we can more accurately call these incidents *signs* or *wonders*. Like the signs cited in John's Gospel that affirmed Jesus as Christ, these signs described in Exodus affirm that Yahweh is God.

As a result of these signs, Pharaoh released the Hebrews from Egyptian bondage, and the Hebrews experienced a newfound freedom. However, the significance of these signs is broader than just the immediate deliverance of the Hebrews. These events signaled

God's adequacy to all of the generations of Hebrews to come. In all three segments of the Hebrew canon—the Law, the Prophets, and the Writings—the biblical writers alluded to these signs as symbols of God's adequacy. Moses alluded to them in one of his speeches recorded in Deuteronomy (Deut. 4:34, in the Law). Jeremiah recalled these signs when affirming the mighty power of God in one of his prayers (Jer. 32:20, in the Prophets). Too, references to these signs appear repeatedly in the Psalms (Psalm 78:12, in the Writings). These signs stand at the bedrock of Hebrew history as unassailable testimony to the awesome power of the covenant God.

The elements of these various signs were not in themselves what we would call miraculous. Plagues often struck down the livestock in Egypt. Flies and gnats were common pests. Frogs were abundant in the Nile River. The dust stirred up by the winds of the desert often blotted out the light of the sun. The elements of these signs were themselves common. What was uncommon, what in fact caught the attention of the Egyptians and eventually Pharaoh himself, was the timing of the events, the intensity

> *Because we know that God is with us today, we too can face the forces of darkness unafraid.*

of the events, and the selectivity of the events. These signs were foretold by Moses and ceased at his command. These signs were severe in their intensity. Too, after the third plague, the plagues affected only the Egyptians but not the Hebrews.

Nine of these signs are identified in our text for this week's lesson. Before we look at the specific signs, let's review the context.

God's Purpose and Pharaoh's Response (7:1–6)

God's purpose in enlisting Moses and initiating the signs in Egypt was not just to deliver the Hebrews. The ultimate purpose of God was to bring glory to himself. The signs would affirm Yahweh's supremacy. The deliverance of Israel would signal Yahweh's sufficiency. When the deliverance occurred, Yahweh declared, "The Egyptians will know that I am the Lord" (7:5).

But Pharaoh would not be convinced easily. Instead of responding to God's initiative, Pharaoh would resist it. "Pharaoh's heart is unyielding," God explained to Moses. "He refuses to let the people go" (7:14).

Paradoxically, the biblical writer would affirm on some occasions that Pharaoh hardened his own heart (8:15, 32; 9:34) and on other occasions that God hardened Pharaoh's heart (7:3; 9:12; 10:1, 20, 27). What does this mean?

The answer to that question is to be found, in part, in the biblical writer's understanding of the sovereign control of God over everything that happens. Therefore, if Pharaoh's heart was hardened, then God must be the one who hardened it, for God never relinquishes his sovereign control. So, the biblical writer concludes: "But the Lord hardened Pharaoh's heart" (9:12).

Nine signs should have been enough to convince Pharaoh.

The answer to that question is also to be found, in part, in the biblical writer's understanding of the moral responsibility of human life. Like Adam and Eve in the Garden of Eden, human beings have the ability to make moral choices and are therefore accountable to God for those moral choices. Therefore, the biblical writer concludes: "But when Pharaoh saw that there was relief, he hardened his heart" (8:15).

The Bible never relieves the tension created by this paradox between human freedom and divine sovereignty. Instead, the Bible explains that the purpose of this hardening of Pharaoh's heart—whether God did it or Pharaoh did it—was to teach the Hebrews in Egyptian captivity and all of the Israelites in the ages to come that God delivered his people in a magnificent way and that his name is to be glorified (Romans 9:17).

The Nine Signs of God's Supremacy (7:14–18; 8:1–3, 16, 20–21; 9:1–4, 8–9, 22–26; 10:3–6, 21–23, 27–29)

The first sign occurred as Pharaoh was going out to the Nile. Pharaoh's daily trip to the Nile River conveys more meaning than first catches the eye (7:15). His daily trip to the Nile was not for exercise or for a bath. Pharaoh was going out for his daily worship of the god of the Nile. So the confrontation, from the very first sign, was between the gods of Egypt and the covenant God. At Moses' command, the water of the Nile was corrupted, for it not only turned red. It became a source of death rather than life. The fish died, and the smell of death emanated from the waters.

The Egyptian magicians duplicated this first sign (7:22), finding some pure water by digging along the shoreline of the river and then

Miracles

The Bible is full of the miraculous. How are we to understand the miracles of the Bible?

One response is to reject them. The scientific age created a mindset that was suspicious of everything that could not be explained on the basis of the scientific method. As we've moved from modernism to post-modernism, the rationalism of the scientific age does not carry the same weight as it did earlier. Yet some continue to respond to miracles with the skepticism of the modern mind.

Another response is to explain miracles in natural terms. In this case, the miraculous elements of the stories are explained away in terms of natural events. For example, the thought is that Jesus fed the 5,000 because he had a supply of food stored in a nearby cave. Too, Jesus' healing miracles were merely psychological manipulation of the psychosomatic illnesses.

A third approach is to realize that miracles can be perceived correctly only through the eyes of faith. Through the eyes of faith we conclude that nothing is beyond the scope of God's power. From this viewpoint, we can discern God at work in our world in extraordinary ways.

---

turning that water red. Consequently, Pharaoh was unmoved by Moses' first sign.

The second sign was a deluge of frogs (8:1–6). As the reference to the Nile included the gods of fertility represented by the river, the reference to frogs went beyond the identification of an animal common to the Egyptian terrain. The frog was associated with the goddess Heqt. This goddess assisted women at childbirth and was, for the Egyptians, a symbol of life-giving power. However, these frogs moved out of the water into the homes of the people, invading every corner of the living areas,

> *Christians today continue to struggle with the paradoxical tension between God's sovereignty and human freedom.*

from the bedrooms to the kitchens. Then they died, adding to the recent stench caused by the dying fish. However, the point was not the stench of the dead frogs but the challenge to another Egyptian god. Instead of being symbols of life, the frogs now became symbols of death.

The Egyptian magicians again duplicated this sign (8:7), for they added to the inundation of frogs by bringing out more frogs. Ironically, they had power only to intensify the problem; they had no power to solve the problem. Pharaoh called on Moses to remove the frogs. If he did,

Pharaoh promised, he would release the Hebrews. However, Pharaoh's promise evaporated as quickly as the frogs disappeared.

So God sent a third sign, empowering Moses to bring out of the dust of the earth an inundation of small insects that covered both human beings and animals (8:16–19). These insects generally are understood to be "gnats," as the word is translated in the New International Version, the New American Standard Bible, and the New Revised Standard Version. The Hebrew word can also refer to lice. Once again, this sign from the Lord challenged the Egyptian value system, for the soil, the source of their food, brought forth instead the invading insects. Pharaoh held firm, refusing to give in to Moses' request.

The fourth sign is identified in our text as "swarms of flies" (8:21). Flies were so common in Egypt that the later prophets used them as a symbol of Egypt (Isaiah 7:18). In this plague, the flies appeared in such huge numbers that they threatened the well-being of the people and their crops. The Bible states, "The houses of the Egyptians will be full of flies" (Exod. 8:21). These flies would fasten themselves on the human body. They would also deposit their eggs in the plants, thus destroying the plant. At this point, God began to distinguish the Hebrews from the Egyptians so that the signs affected only the Egyptians. This distinction provided further evidence that these things were not just coincidences but were instead the workings of the God of Israel. Pharaoh again promised Moses he would let the people leave in order to offer sacrifices to their God. Again, however, Pharaoh reneged on his promise once the threat of the flies was removed.

> "Pray as if everything depends on God, and act as if everything depends on you."

As a result of Pharaoh's continued resistance, God sent yet another sign. This time a plague struck down all of the livestock of Egypt "in the field" (9:1–7). Miraculously, this plague—probably something similar to the anthrax of modern times—did not infect any of the livestock belonging to the Hebrews. Yet Pharaoh was still not convinced.

As a result of Pharaoh's hard heart, God sent yet a sixth sign. This time "festering boils" broke out on people and animals alike (9:9). Two factors remind us that this was not just a display of power but that this sign was also meant to exalt the power of Yahweh over the power of the gods of Egypt. The "handfuls of soot from a furnace" (9:8) was probably the remains of the human sacrifices that were made to propitiate the Egyptian god, Typhon. These sacrifices were made in order to avert plagues that were common in Egypt. In this instance, though, the soot from the sacrifices to avert the plague actually became the source of the plague. Further, the Bible points out that even the spiritual leaders of Egypt were struck by this plague (9:11), another sign of the superiority of Yahweh.

The seventh sign was "the worst hailstorm that has ever fallen on Egypt" (9:19). Thunder and lightning accompanied the hail, wreaking havoc on the land (9:22–26). Plants, animals, and human beings—anything uncovered and unprotected was ripped apart.

When Pharaoh continued to resist Moses' request, insects again swarmed across the land, invading all of the living area, devastating everything in the way (10:1–6). This time the invading insects were locusts. Pharaoh made some concessions, but he imposed limits on these concessions. Only the men could go to worship, not the entire group (10:11). So the locusts came, covering the land so that no one was able to see.

These signs from God convinced the officials of Egypt, but not Pharaoh. He continued to manipulate the situation with his empty promises and insincere concessions.

Christians today also continue to struggle with the conflict between the covenant God and the various gods of our age.

So God sent yet another plague. This time, darkness descended on the land, a darkness that seemed to be tangible. God called it a "darkness that can be felt" (10:21). Since light was the source of life, this darkness that descended on Egypt from the hand of Yahweh, contrasted to the light that still shone on the places where the Hebrews lived, signaled the superiority of Yahweh over the gods of Egypt.

Nine signs should have been enough to convince Pharaoh. Yet, driven by a desire for power and in the grip of greed, he tried to manipulate the situation to his own advantage. Once and for all, God would establish his superiority when the angel of death passed over Egypt. Only then would Pharaoh relent and agree to set God's people free (10:27–29).

Implications for Today

Christians today continue to struggle with the paradoxical tension between God's sovereignty and human freedom. Both ideas run unmistakably throughout the Bible. Neither can be discarded without severely distorting the biblical message. Instead of trying to discern a way to relieve the

Case Study

The members of a Baptist church were disturbed by the announcement that a casino would soon be established in their community. They were convinced that the casino was an evil that would undermine the quality of life in their community. They were equally convinced that God stood in opposition to the introduction of gambling into their community. In what ways could they see and engage God in the issue? What specific activities should they initiate?

tension, perhaps we need to ask ourselves what it means to live within that tension. To acknowledge God's sovereignty, on the one hand, should provide the confidence that God will ultimately work out God's sovereign will. To recognize human freedom, on the other hand, should provide the responsibility to do whatever we can to be a part of God's unfolding sovereign will. The old adage expresses these dual responses in simple terms: "Pray as if everything depends on God, and act as if everything depends on you."

Christians today also continue to struggle with the conflict between the covenant God and the various gods of our age. On one hand, the covenant God, who delivered Israel in the Exodus and provided for our salvation in the life, death, and resurrection of Jesus, calls us to trust in him and consequently to live for him. On the other hand, the gods of this world—popularity, materialism, sensuality, power—call us to give our allegiance to them. What will we do? The reminder of Jesus that we cannot serve the covenant God and the gods of this world at the same time (Matthew 6:24) is not so much a statement of ethical demand as it is a declaration of spiritual impossibility. We ultimately have to choose whom we will serve.

We ultimately have to choose whom we will serve.

QUESTIONS

1. What has God called you to do?

2. What deliberate choices have you made that will enable you to fulfill that calling?

3. In what ways have you hardened your heart against the purposes of God?

4. What signs has God given you in your life that reflect God's power over the forces of evil?

5. Why are we so hesitant to trust God and to fulfill God's purpose in our lives?

6. What are some of the gods that call you away from allegiance to the covenant God?

Focal Text
Exodus 11:1–8; 12:21–32

Background
Exodus 11:1—13:16

Main Idea
God's overwhelming power brings joy to those who respond to God and tragedy to those who refuse God.

Question to Explore
When children ask what this is all about, what will you say?

Study Aim
To summarize the final plague and its meaning and to recall God's gracious acts on my behalf

Study and Action Emphases

- Affirm the Bible as our authoritative guide for life and ministry
- Share the gospel with all people
- Develop a growing, vibrant faith

LESSON FOUR

A Night Never to Be Forgotten

Quick Read
At long last, the Hebrew slaves were released from their captivity. They recognized their freedom had come because of the gracious provision of God.

The owner of the shop where my wife Jan bought her makeup bombarded Jan each time she stopped by with the latest amazing feats of her new grandchild. This little bundle of joy was the center of the family's attention. One day, though, when Jan made her regular stop, the owner announced that the baby had inexplicably died. Tears flowed as she unfolded the details. On the day the baby died, the baby's mother left the hospital and exploded with anguish, looking up to the heavens shouting, "I want a sign. I want a sign." In that moment a beautiful rainbow broke across the sky. This distraught mother found comfort in this reminder of the power and presence of God.

After decades of affliction as slaves in Egypt, the Hebrews longed for such a sign. God didn't give them a rainbow. Instead, God brought them out of their bondage and sent them toward their Promised Land in a night never to be forgotten.

Exodus 11:1–8

¹Now the LORD had said to Moses, "I will bring one more plague on Pharaoh and on Egypt. After that, he will let you go from here, and when he does, he will drive you out completely. ²Tell the people that men and women alike are to ask their neighbors for articles of silver and gold." ³(The LORD made the Egyptians favorably disposed toward the people, and Moses himself was highly regarded in Egypt by Pharaoh's officials and by the people.)

⁴So Moses said, "This is what the LORD says: 'About midnight I will go throughout Egypt. ⁵Every firstborn son in Egypt will die, from the firstborn son of Pharaoh, who sits on the throne, to the firstborn son of the slave girl, who is at her hand mill, and all the firstborn of the cattle as well. ⁶There will be loud wailing throughout Egypt—worse than there has ever been or ever will be again. ⁷But among the Israelites not a dog will bark at any man or animal.' Then you will know that the LORD makes a distinction between Egypt and Israel. ⁸All these officials of yours will come to me, bowing down before me and saying, 'Go, you and all the people who follow you!' After that I will leave." Then Moses, hot with anger, left Pharaoh.

Exodus 12:21–32

²¹Then Moses summoned all the elders of Israel and said to them, "Go at once and select the animals for your families and slaughter the Passover

lamb. [22] Take a bunch of hyssop, dip it into the blood in the basin and put some of the blood on the top and on both sides of the doorframe. Not one of you shall go out the door of his house until morning. [23] When the LORD goes through the land to strike down the Egyptians, he will see the blood on the top and sides of the doorframe and will pass over that doorway, and he will not permit the destroyer to enter your houses and strike you down.

[24] "Obey these instructions as a lasting ordinance for you and your descendants. [25] When you enter the land that the LORD will give you as he promised, observe this ceremony. [26] And when your children ask you, 'What does this ceremony mean to you?' [27] then tell them, 'It is the Passover sacrifice to the LORD, who passed over the houses of the Israelites in Egypt and spared our homes when he struck down the Egyptians.'" Then the people bowed down and worshiped. [28] The Israelites did just what the LORD commanded Moses and Aaron.

[29] At midnight the LORD struck down all the firstborn in Egypt, from the firstborn of Pharaoh, who sat on the throne, to the firstborn of the prisoner, who was in the dungeon, and the firstborn of all the livestock as well. [30] Pharaoh and all his officials and all the Egyptians got up during the night, and there was loud wailing in Egypt, for there was not a house without someone dead.

[31] During the night Pharaoh summoned Moses and Aaron and said, "Up! Leave my people, you and the Israelites! Go, worship the LORD as you have requested. [32] Take your flocks and herds, as you have said, and go. And also bless me."

Background of the Biblical Story

We studied in last week's lesson the nine signs God sent to affirm his superiority over the gods of Egypt and to convince Pharaoh to let his people go. Even though Pharaoh would weaken at times and make concessions to Moses and to the Hebrews, he would quickly relent. As a result, the plight of the Hebrews was the same. They still languished as slaves under the control of the Egyptians. So God sent one more sign. The death angel passed over Egypt, claiming the firstborn of every family and the firstborn of the cattle as well. Because of God's instructions Moses gave to the Hebrews, the death angel passed over them. Not one child among the Hebrews was taken.

From that action of the death angel passing over the Hebrews comes the name given to this special night in all of the succeeding history of the

Jews. This was Passover night. Passover became the first and the most important historically and religiously of all the annual feasts. This feast commemorated the deliverance of the Hebrews from Egypt and the establishment of Israel as a nation by God's redemptive act.

Israel was given explicit instructions on how to keep the Passover, reenacting each year Israel's preparations for leaving Egypt. The centerpiece of the celebration was killing the paschal lamb. At times, God's people neglected to celebrate the Passover. However, in times of revival, the people would reestablish the Passover as a reminder of God's deliverance.

How did the Passover happen? Further, what was the meaning of the Passover celebration? We find answers to those questions in this week's lesson.

Moses' Defiant Encounter with Pharaoh (11:1–8)

Before Moses met with Pharaoh, he met with God. God announced to Moses that he would send one more "plague" on Egypt. Although we find the same English word here that was used in Exodus 9:3 ("plague"), the Hebrew word is different. The Hebrew word here in Exodus 11:1 means *a blow* or *a stroke*, depicting the impact this final sign would have on the leaders of Egypt. In preparation for the event that would unfold after this final blow on Egypt, Moses instructed the people to "ask their neighbors for articles of silver and gold" (Exodus 11:2). As God promised Moses in his burning bush experience (Exod. 3:21–22), the Egyptians responded to the Hebrews' request with generosity (12:35–36).

Why would the Egyptians respond generously to this kind of request from the Hebrew slaves? The Bible suggests two motivations: the divine nudging of God and the high respect the Egyptians had for Moses (11:3). Two other motivations can be discerned from the context. Perhaps the Egyptians were afraid to refuse the Hebrews' request after having observed the devastating outpouring of Yahweh's power. In this case, fear was the motive. Or maybe Pharaoh's consistent persecution of the Hebrews generated a sympathetic response from the people. In this case, guilt was the motive. Whatever motivated them, the response of the Egyptians was lavish.

"I want a sign. I want a sign."

The central theme of this passage, however, is not the generosity of the Egyptians to the response of the Hebrews but the dramatic encounter between the leader of the Hebrews and the leader of the Egyptians. Armed with the authority of God and carrying the message of God, Moses appeared one last time before Pharaoh. Perhaps Pharaoh was skeptical when he heard the latest announcement from Moses, for Moses promised that a death angel would sweep across the land, striking down the firstborn of every family, including

By honoring God and by obeying God, the Hebrews expressed their gratitude for the blessed deliverance God gave them.

Pharaoh's firstborn. How could such a thing happen! The Pharaoh was no doubt skeptical. Nevertheless, his skepticism would soon be swallowed up by a wave of despair as the death angel moved across Egypt, leaving behind a wake of death. The fulfillment of this tragic proclamation by God waited as Moses prepared the Hebrew people for what was to come.

The Obedient Response of the Hebrews (12:21–28)

The death angel was to wreak havoc on the Egyptian people. The Hebrews, however, would be spared, because the death angel would pass over them.

Moses gave the people instructions on how they could prepare for the coming death angel. In so doing, Moses provided the basic pattern for the

The Lord's Supper

In Baptist life, we have often de-emphasized the Lord's Supper by relegating it to only a quarterly observance or by tagging it on to the end of a regular worship service and hurrying through it. Instead of neglecting the Lord's Supper, we should make it a central part of our worship experience. We should do this, not because the bread and the juice actually become the body of Christ, but because the bread and the juice are tangible symbols to remind us of the sacrifice Jesus made on our behalf on the cross and to remind us of the eventual consummation of this age when Jesus returns.

Instead of hurrying through the observance of the meal, we should allow enough time for the true meaning of the symbols to take hold of our minds. The bread and the cup help us to remember what God has done for us in our past and what God has in store for us in our future. We need regularly to remember those things.

Passover celebration that would play such a central part in the future history of Israel. The Passover meal would feature a lamb that was to be eaten with unleavened bread and bitter herbs (12:8). Each of these elements would remind the participants in the meal of the experience on that first Passover night. The roast lamb would symbolize the lamb that was slain and the blood that was spread on the door to spare their firstborn from the death angel. The unleavened bread would symbolize the haste with which the Hebrews had to leave Egypt. They left so quickly that they did not even have time to leaven the bread in the normal way. The bitter herbs would symbolize the hard times the Hebrews had as they suffered in Egypt.

The beginning of this Passover tradition is found in the events of Israel's last night in Egypt, but on that night these events served a very practical purpose. The blood from the Passover lamb, smeared on their doorframe, would protect the Hebrews and their families from the death angel. Each family was to slaughter the Passover lamb. The hyssop, which was a bushy plant, would serve as a brush to spread the blood on the doorframe. The focus on that first Passover night was not the meal featuring the Passover lamb but the blood itself.

In the following years, however, the Passover lamb would become the centerpiece of a memorial meal that would remind each new generation of the extraordinary night when God delivered their ancestors from their Egyptian bondage. The annual celebration would provide a teaching time for the parents. The children would be given the opportunity to ask questions. To these questions, the parents would provide answers that would explain the meaning of the Passover celebration. Notice how succinctly Moses expressed the significance of this event: "It is the Passover sacrifice to the LORD, who passed over the houses of the Israelites in Egypt and spared our homes when he struck down the Egyptians" (12:27).

The Bible emphasizes the urgency of Pharaoh's actions.

The relationship of the instructions concerning the Passover (12:1–11) to the instructions concerning the Feast of Unleavened Bread (12:17–20) is somewhat hard to understand, for the Feast of Unleavened Bread and the Passover were actually two different feasts. The Feast of Unleavened Bread followed the celebration of the Passover. Both feasts, however, celebrated God's deliverance of Israel from Egyptian slavery. The Feast of Unleavened Bread focused more on the haste with which God brought the Israelites out of Egypt. They did not even have time to leaven their bread.

How did the Hebrews respond to God's instructions concerning the Passover celebration delivered to them through Moses? They first of all worshiped God (12:27). To worship is to give honor to, and they gave honor to God because they realized that they would be delivered because of the unmerited favor of God. Then they obeyed God (12:28). Hearing the word of God is not enough. Even believing the word of God is not enough. We must be willing to obey the word of God. Later writers would also emphasize the importance of obedience (Jeremiah 11:3; Daniel 9:4; John 14:15; 1 John 2:3). By honoring God and by obeying God, the Hebrews expressed their gratitude for the blessed deliverance God gave them.

The Anguish of the Egyptians (12:29–32)

Having responded obediently to God's command given through Moses, the Hebrews were *prepared* for what was to come. However, they were probably not *ready*. Who could ever be ready for such a sweep of tragedy and such a depth of sorrow? No Egyptian family was spared, no matter how low or how high on the social scale. Every family was included. Death struck indiscriminately at the hand of the angel of death. One by one, the death angel struck down the eldest

The events described in this lesson remind us how important it is to remember.

sons of the Egyptian families. As the news spread from house to house, echoes of wailing filled the night air. Just as the Hebrews had wailed in their suffering through generations of slavery (Exod. 3:7, 9), even so the Egyptians now wailed in their suffering on that never to be forgotten night (11:6).

At this point, Pharaoh joined the rest of the Egyptians in their desire for the Hebrews to leave. He not only allowed them to leave; he compelled them to leave. No more hesitancy. No more limitations. The Bible emphasizes the urgency of Pharaoh's actions. It was "at midnight" when the death angel swept through the land, taking the firstborn of all the Egyptian families (12:29). It was "during the night" when the Pharaoh decided something had to be done (12:30). It was "during the night" that Pharaoh summoned Moses and Aaron into his presence (12:31), even though he had earlier told Moses he would never see his face again (10:28). *Take your flocks. Take your people. All of them, and go!* Pharaoh cried. He moved with urgency lest some greater disaster would strike his people.

The central theme of this passage, however, is not on Pharaoh and his actions but on the actions of God and on what God's actions meant religiously for the Hebrew people. What happened that night in Egypt was not just the defeat of Pharaoh. This was a defeat of the gods of Egypt.

The events described in this lesson . . . remind us how important it is to celebrate.

Pharaoh was powerless to retain the Hebrews. He was powerless to protect his people, even his own family. He was powerless to resist the awesome power of Yahweh. What God clearly declared in Exodus 12:12 where God explained that the blow from the death angel will "bring judgment on all the gods of Egypt" is implied in the pathetic whimper of Pharaoh as he asked the departing Moses: "And also bless me" (12:32). Pharaoh himself briefly acknowledged the supremacy of the God of Israel.

Implications for Today

The events described in this lesson remind us how important it is to remember. Repeating the rituals of the Passover meal each year would stimulate the memory of the Hebrews, for they would remember again God's remarkable deliverance of their ancestors (12:25–27). When Jesus transformed the Passover meal into the Lord's Supper, he suggested this same note of remembrance. "Do this," Jesus told the disciples, "in

Symbols

Use this week's lesson as a springboard for considering some of the symbols of life in our day.

- Spend some time identifying the significant symbols from the different dimensions of life. You might consider symbols in the realm of family life or the educational institutions you have been a part of or even the national scene.

- Then, concentrate on some of the important symbols in the religious dimension of your life. Discuss ways to focus more intentionally on these religious symbols and their meaning.

remembrance of me" (1 Corinthians 11:24). Whenever we take the cup and eat the bread, we remember what God has done for us in Jesus Christ.

The events described in this lesson also remind us how important it is to celebrate. The purpose of the Passover meal was to remember what God had done for Israel. Whenever we remember what God has done for us in Jesus Christ, we are to celebrate with thanksgiving his undeserved and unmeasured blessings.

> *. . . The events described in this lesson remind us how important it is to obey.*

Further, the events described in this lesson remind us how important it is to obey. Recognizing the importance of the instructions God was giving them through their leader Moses, the Hebrew people did exactly what God commanded them to do (Exod. 12:28, 50). Remembering what God has done for us through Jesus Christ and celebrating the unparalleled graciousness of God to us, how can we do anything except obey God's commands?

QUESTIONS

1. Remember your conversion experience. Who were the people who influenced you in that decision?

2. Remember a time when you experienced God's presence in an unusual way. What did you learn about God in that experience? What did you learn about yourself?

3. Remember some of the extraordinary blessings God has given to you. Have you thanked God for them lately?

4. Remember how God expects you to live as a Christian. Are you fulfilling God's expectations each day?

5. Remember the individuals God has placed in your life to give you encouragement and guidance. Have you expressed your gratitude to them recently?

Focal Text

Exodus 14:21—
15:2, 20–21

Background

Exodus 13:17—15:21

Main Idea

We can rejoice in God's powerful acts in providing us victory over life's difficulties and all that enslaves us.

Question to Explore

What puts a song in your heart?

Study Aim

To identify God's blessings in my life and express joyful gratitude to God for them

Study and Action Emphases

- Affirm the Bible as our authoritative guide for life and ministry
- Share the gospel with all people
- Develop a growing, vibrant faith

LESSON FIVE

Sing to the Lord for Freedom!

Quick Read

A quick review of our lives will reflect the richness of our blessings from God. The only proper response to the graciousness of God is gratitude.

57

Billy's parents experienced the horror that all parents fear—an incident in which they almost lost the life of their son. It happened so quickly that the danger was over almost before they realized the danger was there. Billy was sitting in the back seat of the car and had forgotten to put on his seatbelt. When the father took a left turn, Billy, sitting on the passenger side, accidentally opened the door and the door swung open. Billy somehow hung on to the armrest and the back of the seat in front of him until his father had stopped the car. Billy's parents breathed a sigh of relief when they discovered their precious son was safe. That night, as Billy's mother put him to bed, she suggested that he say a prayer of thanks to God for saving him. Billy responded, "Why should I thank God? I'm the one who hung on."

At times, Israel adopted that attitude toward their blessings. Instead of thanking God, they patted themselves on the back. But not in the incident described in our text. God's hand was so evidently present that they could not mistake the source of their mighty deliverance. Their deliverance was undeniably an act of the God of the covenant. In response to the magnificent act of God in their lives, Moses and Miriam led the people in a celebrative song of thanksgiving.

Exodus 14:21–31

21Then Moses stretched out his hand over the sea, and all that night the LORD drove the sea back with a strong east wind and turned it into dry land. The waters were divided, 22and the Israelites went through the sea on dry ground, with a wall of water on their right and on their left.

23The Egyptians pursued them, and all Pharaoh's horses and chariots and horsemen followed them into the sea. 24During the last watch of the night the LORD looked down from the pillar of fire and cloud at the Egyptian army and threw it into confusion. 25He made the wheels of their chariots come off so that they had difficulty driving. And the Egyptians said, "Let's get away from the Israelites! The LORD is fighting for them against Egypt."

26Then the LORD said to Moses, "Stretch out your hand over the sea so that the waters may flow back over the Egyptians and their chariots and horsemen." 27Moses stretched out his hand over the sea, and at daybreak the sea went back to its place. The Egyptians were fleeing toward it, and the LORD swept them into the sea. 28The water flowed back and covered the chariots and horsemen—the entire army of Pharaoh that had followed the Israelites into the sea. Not one of them survived.

²⁹But the Israelites went through the sea on dry ground, with a wall of water on their right and on their left. ³⁰That day the LORD saved Israel from the hands of the Egyptians, and Israel saw the Egyptians lying dead on the shore. ³¹And when the Israelites saw the great power the LORD displayed against the Egyptians, the people feared the LORD and put their trust in him and in Moses his servant.

Exodus 15:1–2, 20–21

¹Then Moses and the Israelites sang this song to the LORD:
"I will sing to the LORD,
for he is highly exalted.
The horse and its rider
he has hurled into the sea.
² The LORD is my strength and my song;
he has become my salvation.
He is my God, and I will praise him,
my father's God, and I will exalt him.

· · · · · · · · · · · · · · · · · ·

²⁰Then Miriam the prophetess, Aaron's sister, took a tambourine in her hand, and all the women followed her, with tambourines and dancing. ²¹Miriam sang to them:
"Sing to the LORD,
for he is highly exalted.
The horse and its rider
he has hurled into the sea."

Background of the Biblical Story

As they departed from Egypt under the leadership of Moses, the Hebrews could have taken three different routes. The quickest and most direct route would have taken them northeast, through the land indwelled by the Philistines, and directly into Canaan. Or they could have headed directly east, toward Beersheba, and then into Canaan from the south. Or they could take a southeast route leading through the Sinai Peninsula and eventually into Canaan from the southeast.

God specifically warned Israel not to take the shorter route through the area of the Philistines, for facing the Philistines at this point would have demoralized them (Exodus 13:17). But how would they decide between the middle route and the more southern route? God directed them with a "pillar" (Exod. 14:24), which was a cloud by day and a fire by night. Following the "pillar," the masses of Hebrews recently released from their Egyptian bondage headed southeast toward the Sinai Peninsula and toward the Red Sea, which can also be translated as Sea of Reeds (13:18).

"Why should I thank God? I'm the one who hung on."

The Hebrews seem to have been in some confusion at this point. As it turned out, however, this confusion would serve God's purpose. Pharaoh by this point had decided he had made a mistake to let the Hebrew slaves go. As he pursued them, he would evaluate what appeared to be the Hebrews' confusion as a false note of hope. This false note of hope would draw Pharaoh into the trap God was setting for the Egyptians. Their ultimate defeat would signify Yahweh's superiority over the gods of Egypt.

When the Hebrews realized that Pharaoh and his armies were pursuing them, their mood was not one of confidence but instead one of despair. We cannot imagine the depth of the anguish of the Hebrews when they heard the sound of the Egyptian army in hot pursuit of them. This anguish was deepened when the waters of the sea blocked the pathway ahead. Out of their panic, they cried out to God and condemned Moses, all in the same breath (14:10–11). Their lack of confidence was the product of years of enslavement in Egypt. However, Moses was not afraid, for God had promised him victory over the Egyptians. Too, in this victory, God would accomplish what all of the plagues had not accomplished. "The Egyptians will know that I am the LORD," God told Moses, "when I gain glory through Pharaoh, his chariots and his horsemen" (14:18). The victory was not the *result* of the faith of the Israelites. Instead, it became the *source* of faith through the centuries, as their ancestors recounted over and over again the mighty deliverance of God. As one example, the prophet Isaiah later said: "When you pass through the waters, I will be with you; and when you pass through the rivers, they will not sweep over you. . . . For I am the LORD, your God, the Holy One of Israel, your Savior" (Isaiah 43:2–3).

The Mighty Deliverance of God (14:21–31)

As the Egyptians pressed down on the Hebrews, Moses sprang into action. He was the human leader as the Hebrews moved through the Red Sea, but

The Names of God

To distinguish the God of Israel from the gods of the other nations, the biblical writers used specific names to identify God. Some of the names illuminated God's attributes; others described God's actions.

In Exodus 15:2, the word translated "he," referring to God, is the Hebrew word *el*, which was a more widely used word for God than *Yahweh*. The predominant name given to God in Moses' song of celebration, however, is *Yahweh*, the covenant name for God. The NIV translates this word with the English word "LORD."

Based on God's revelation to Moses in the burning bush experience (Exod. 3), the focus on the covenant God is understandable. Yet, this was only one of several names used to identify God in the Old Testament. Noting the different names used for God in the biblical witness is important because the Old Testament concept of God is developed by these words or phrases. The various names for God set the God of Israel apart from other competing deities. In these descriptive names, the true God is gradually revealed to us.

---

the biblical text reminds us in several ways that God was present on the side of Israel. God was present in the pillar of cloud and fire (14:24). The angel of God also represented God's presence with God's people (14:19).

God opened a way through the sea so that the Hebrews could escape from the clutches of the Egyptians. Notice the combination of what we call the natural and supernatural in the parting of the waters. When Moses stretched out his hand, the water divided (14:16–17). At the same time, God caused a strong wind to blow and drive back the waters of the sea (14:21).

When the Hebrews realized that Pharaoh and his armies were pursuing them, their mood was not one of confidence but instead one of despair.

With a passageway open in front of them, the Hebrews followed Moses to the other side, with a wall of water on either side. By this time, the Egyptians were also approaching the sea. Noticing the passageway that had been opened, they pursued the Hebrews in their chariots. Ironically, what had been their greatest advantage in warfare—their chariots—in this instance became a liability. The seabed was apparently dry enough for the Hebrews to walk across but not dry enough to support the heavy chariots.

When the chariots bogged down, the Egyptians became confused. Notice again the combination of the ordinary and the extraordinary.

The Egyptian chariots mired in the mud in a natural way. However, the Egyptians interpreted their dilemma by referring to the Hebrews' God.

Recognizing that they were once more pitted against the God of Israel, the Egyptians tried to escape. By this time, though, it was too late. Moses again lifted his staff over the water. This time, as if a dam had burst, the walls of water collapsed on the Egyptians, and they were drowned in the sudden surge of water. Although natural elements were involved in the battle—the wind that helped to part the water and the mud that wreaked such havoc on the Egyptian chariots—God orchestrated the victory.

> *Although natural elements were involved in the battle . . . God orchestrated the victory.*

The recognition of the greatness of the God of Israel by the Egyptians signaled their doom (14:25). The recognition of the greatness of God by the Israelites solidified their faith (14:31). In a burst of inspiration, Moses articulated Israel's faith in God with a song of victory.

Moses' Song of Victory (15:1–2)

Moses' song of victory covers eighteen verses and recounts the extraordinary events described in Exodus 14. Verses 4–12 of Exodus 15 provide the details of God's deliverance of Israel. Then, using a metaphor that weaves through the entire Bible—the metaphor of a shepherd who provides for his sheep—Moses pictured God's provision for his people (15:13). The verses in our focal text announce the keynote of the song. This is a song of celebration. It is a hymn of praise to God for God's deliverance. Too, it is an announcement to the world of the unparalleled greatness of the God of Israel.

Worship

Worship is a "hot button" among many Christians today. The descriptive term "worship wars" indicates the intensity of the debate. Most often, the debate centers around various styles of worship. In the Bible, the issue more commonly revolves around attitudes toward worship. The key to worship is the celebrative mood that focuses on God and acknowledges God's goodness. Consider and prepare to discuss with your class how that *attitude* toward worship can be reflected in different *styles* of worship.

Moses presented God as the One who empowers his people. "The LORD is my strength," Moses declared (15:2). The psalmist would later echo the words of Moses, identifying God as "my strength and my song" (Psalm 118:14). Isaiah repeated the pronouncement of Moses as he also reminded his generation that, "The LORD, the LORD, is my strength and my song" (Isa. 12:2). The word "strength" reflects the power with which God assists his people.

Moses presented God as the one who saves his people. "He has become my salvation," Moses declared (Exod. 15:2). "Salvation" suggests the whole process of God's mighty acts, including God's judgment on the adversaries and God's assistance to his children (see also Jeremiah 3:23; Lamentations 3:26).

In addition, Moses presented God as the one who inspires his people. "The Lord is . . . my song," Moses declared (Exod. 15:2). Other than Psalm 118:14 and Isaiah 12:2, which are duplicates of Exodus 15:2, no other Old Testament writer refers to God as "my song." The reference that provides the closest parallel is found in Psalm 40:3: "He put a new song in my mouth, a hymn of praise to our God." God gives us a reason to sing. He inspires a joy for life. He is our "song."

> *God gives us a reason to sing.*

Moses also presented God as the one who fights for his people. "The Lord is a warrior," Moses declared (Exod. 15:3). The connection of this word "warrior" with God is not common in the Old Testament. Yet the theme of God's intervention on behalf of God's people runs throughout the Old Testament.

When Moses focused on such a great God as the God of Israel—a God who strengthens his people, saves his people, inspires his people, and fights for his people—we should not be surprised to hear him sing: "He is my God, and I will praise him, my Father's God, and I will exalt him" (15:2).

Miriam's Song of Victory (15:19–21)

Following Moses' song of victory, Miriam led the women in a song of victory. The succinct summary of the song in verse 21 is almost a duplicate of the opening verse of Moses' song. So no new theme is introduced. Some suggest that this was simply an antiphonal response that the women repeated at the conclusion of each part of a longer song, either the song of Moses just recorded or the song of Miriam that is not recorded. Perhaps it is more important to recognize the actions that accompanied the song—the dancing of the women accompanied by the tambourine. Their actions reflect the enthusiasm with which the people praised God for God's mighty deliverance.

Perhaps the other factor worth noting is the identification of Miriam as a "prophetess" (15:20). Apparently, Miriam was a spokesperson for the Lord on some occasions. This role for Miriam seems to be confirmed by Numbers 12:1–2. Or perhaps the title reflects her leadership role in Israel as a sister of Moses and Aaron. This role for Miriam seems to be confirmed by Micah 6:4. Miriam, like other women identified as prophetesses (Deborah in Judges 4:4, Huldah in 2 Kings 22:14, and Isaiah's wife in Isaiah 8:3), provided leadership to Israel in a period of masculine preeminence. In the aftermath of God's deliverance of Israel, Miriam too sang a song of praise to the God of Israel.

Implications for Today

In many churches today, the celebrative, joyful note of Moses' and Miriam's songs is missing. One little boy asked his father on the way home from church, "Are you happy, Daddy?" The father responded, "Yes, son. I'm happy." To which the boy responded, "Don't you think you should tell your face?"

Paul told us to "rejoice in the Lord always" (Philippians 4:4). Yet today many Christians look as if they are headed to a funeral instead of living from a resurrection. They act as if they are still in bondage instead of celebrating their freedom through Christ. We have lost the note of joyful celebration.

. . . The theme of God's intervention on behalf of God's people runs throughout the Old Testament.

In many Christian lives today, the grateful note of Moses' and Miriam's songs is also missing. A mother asked her child as she put him to bed, "Have you said your prayers tonight?" To which the child responded, "No, I don't need anything tonight."

Paul urges us to "give thanks in all circumstances" (1 Thessalonians 5:18). Yet today many Christians seem to take life for granted rather than taking it with gratitude. They act as if they have nothing to be thankful for. We have lost the note of gracious thanksgiving.

Perhaps it is time to sing a new song in our churches—a song of celebration and joy, a song of gratitude and thanksgiving.

QUESTIONS

1. Why do we neglect joyful celebration in our worship? Is it because of fear? propriety? a feeling of insecurity? a lack of perception of God's blessings in our lives?

2. What are the things that bring a smile to your face and a song to your heart?

3. What circumstances in your life dilute your sense of gratitude? How can you correct your perspective on these circumstances?

4. What words do you connect with God? What images come to mind when you think of God?

Focal Text

Exodus 15:22—
16:7; 17:1–7

Background

Exodus 15:22—18:27

Main Idea

Rather than seeking
anxiously to force God to
conform to our desires,
we can trust God to
provide for our needs.

Question to Explore

"Is the Lord among
us or not?"

Study Aim

To describe how God provided for the Hebrews'
needs and state lessons from these events for
dealing with our own difficulties and desires

Study and Action Emphases

- Affirm the Bible as our authoritative guide
  for life and ministry
- Develop a growing, vibrant faith
- Obey and serve Jesus by meeting physical,
  spiritual, and emotional needs

LESSON SIX

No Longer but Not Yet

Quick Read

Life constantly confronts us with challenges that
are beyond our capacity. However, God is always
sufficient to meet all of the needs of his people, if
we will trust him.

Years have passed since this tragic event in one of the families in my church, and yet the incident remains one of the clearest examples of faith in the midst of difficult times. A fire broke out in the home of Hong and Su Dang, leaders in our Vietnamese Ministry at First Baptist Church, Pensacola, Florida. All of the family members escaped safely except their baby girl, who was a fatality of this tragic fire.

When I made my way over to the house to visit with the family, I was not sure what I would say. Surprisingly, it was not I who comforted the family but Hong who comforted me. "If I have my house but do not have Jesus," he told me, "I have nothing. And if I have my health, but do not have Jesus, I have nothing. And if I have my family, but do not have Jesus, I have nothing. But," he added, "if I have Jesus, no matter what else happens to me, I have everything."

Unfortunately, many times, faith does not shine as brightly in the midst of fiery trials as it did in the lives of Hong and Su Dang. Instead, it dissolves into cynicism and doubt. As a case in point, think about the recently delivered Hebrew slaves who wandered through the wilderness on the way to their Promised Land. Each setback stirred up a barrage of complaints, directed at Moses and at times also directed at God.

Exodus 15:22–27

[22]Then Moses led Israel from the Red Sea and they went into the Desert of Shur. For three days they traveled in the desert without finding water. [23]When they came to Marah, they could not drink its water because it was bitter. (That is why the place is called Marah.) [24]So the people grumbled against Moses, saying, "What are we to drink?"

[25]Then Moses cried out to the LORD, and the LORD showed him a piece of wood. He threw it into the water, and the water became sweet.

There the LORD made a decree and a law for them, and there he tested them. [26]He said, "If you listen carefully to the voice of the LORD your God and do what is right in his eyes, if you pay attention to his commands and keep all his decrees, I will not bring on you any of the diseases I brought on the Egyptians, for I am the LORD, who heals you."

[27]Then they came to Elim, where there were twelve springs and seventy palm trees, and they camped there near the water.

Exodus 16:1–7

[1]The whole Israelite community set out from Elim and came to the Desert of Sin, which is between Elim and Sinai, on the fifteenth day of the second month after they had come out of Egypt. [2]In the desert the whole community grumbled against Moses and Aaron. [3]The Israelites said to them, "If only we had died by the LORD's hand in Egypt! There we sat around pots of meat and ate all the food we wanted, but you have brought us out into this desert to starve this entire assembly to death."

[4]Then the LORD said to Moses, "I will rain down bread from heaven for you. The people are to go out each day and gather enough for that day. In this way I will test them and see whether they will follow my instructions. [5]On the sixth day they are to prepare what they bring in, and that is to be twice as much as they gather on the other days."

[6]So Moses and Aaron said to all the Israelites, "In the evening you will know that it was the LORD who brought you out of Egypt, [7]and in the morning you will see the glory of the LORD, because he has heard your grumbling against him. Who are we, that you should grumble against us?"

Exodus 17:1–7

[1]The whole Israelite community set out from the Desert of Sin, traveling from place to place as the LORD commanded. They camped at Rephidim, but there was no water for the people to drink. [2]So they quarreled with Moses and said, "Give us water to drink."

Moses replied, "Why do you quarrel with me? Why do you put the LORD to the test?"

[3]But the people were thirsty for water there, and they grumbled against Moses. They said, "Why did you bring us up out of Egypt to make us and our children and livestock die of thirst?"

[4]Then Moses cried out to the LORD, "What am I to do with these people? They are almost ready to stone me."

[5]The LORD answered Moses, "Walk on ahead of the people. Take with you some of the elders of Israel and take in your hand the staff with which you struck the Nile, and go. [6]I will stand there before you by the rock at Horeb. Strike the rock, and water will come out of it for the people to drink." So Moses did this in the sight of the elders of Israel. [7]And he called the place Massah and Meribah because the Israelites quarreled and because they tested the LORD saying, "Is the LORD among us or not?"

Background of the Biblical Story

After the Hebrews' triumphant deliverance from Egypt and their song of victory recorded in Exodus 15, we would expect the following days to be punctuated with continued celebration and pervaded by completed confidence in God. Instead, we see that Moses had almost as much trouble with the Hebrews in the wilderness as he did with Pharaoh in Egypt. Instead of reaching forward to the things ahead, the recently delivered captives longed for the things left behind. Instead of trusting God with their future, they longed for the good old days that never were. Instead of celebrating, they constantly complained.

" . . . If I have Jesus, no matter what else happens to me, I have everything."

The journey from Egypt to Sinai, recorded in Exodus 15—18, was marked at each step along the way by dissension and despair. In each case, God showed his sufficiency to address the need and overcome the challenge presented by the Hebrew people.

At Marah in the Desert of Shur (15:22–26)

The journey toward Sinai, where the Hebrews would have their dramatic encounter with the Holy God and would receive from him the laws of the covenant, first took them eastward from Egypt into the desert of Shur (called the desert of Etham in Numbers 33:8). Both Shur and Etham mean *fortress wall*. Some scholars identify this *fortress wall* as a line of frontier fortresses built to the east of Egypt as a buffer against invading forces. Other scholars identify this *fortress wall* as a range of white cliffs parallel to the Mediterranean coast.

The crisis arose from a water supply that could not be utilized because it was "bitter." Hence, the place was known as "Marah," which means "bitter" (15:23). The complaint of the people is easy to understand. For three days they had traveled in the desert. They were thirsty. What would they drink? They came upon a source of water, but their celebration turned to complaint when they discovered the water was too bitter to drink. So their concern is understandable. However, the tone of their complaint reflected a criticism of Moses' leadership and an uncertainty about God's provision.

Moses turned to God for relief, and God provided a solution. Notice that God did not transform the water miraculously. He did it naturally, and he used Moses to accomplish this needed provision of water. Moses threw a particular kind of wood into the water, removing the bitterness so that the people could now drink the water. Some scholars suggest that Moses learned about the counteracting power of this particular kind of wood during his forty years in the wilderness, and that this was simply another part of God's preparation. The text, however, suggests that God directed Moses to this particular kind of tree at this moment of crisis.

Each setback stirred up a barrage of complaints, directed at Moses and at times also directed at God.

God apparently used this incident as an object lesson. By the same power with which God cleansed the water of its uncleanness, God would spare the Hebrew people of the diseases that had struck down the Egyptians. What God demanded of them was obedience to his commands. This idea, introduced to the Hebrews in the Desert of Shur, would become the definitive guideline of God's covenant relationship with his people. Their obedience would bring God's blessings. On the other hand, their disobedience would call forth God's judgment.

Manna

The strange bread in the wilderness known as manna has stirred scholarly curiosity across the years. "What is it?" the Hebrews asked when they first saw it (Exodus 16:15).

Scholars have been asking the same question ever since. Some have identified the manna with a honey-like substance produced by the tamarisk tree. The substance drips to the ground and turns white as it crystallizes. Others have identified the manna with the secretion of certain insects.

Neither of these answers, however, fits with the characteristics of manna given in the Scripture. The manna was provided in abundant supplies every day (except the Sabbath) for forty years. Even though different individuals collected different amounts, what they collected was always sufficient. The manna did not appear on the Sabbath. Further, if kept until morning, the manna putrefied. None of these characteristics fits either the substance secreted by the tamarisk tree or the secretion of the desert insects.

Moses' explanation is the best. He simply called the manna "the bread the Lord has given you" (16:15).

At Elim in the Wilderness of Sin (15:27—16:7)

After the experience at Marah, the Hebrews moved in a more southerly direction and came to a place called Elim. Ironically, the shortage of water at Marah was matched by the abundance of water at Elim, for the Bible says the Hebrews found "twelve springs and seventy palm trees" at Elim. Both "twelve" and "seventy" are significant numbers in the biblical story of Israel, and so perhaps the numbers are figurative. In any case, the biblical text acknowledges an abundance of resources that satisfied the thirst of the people.

However, we notice two things about the Hebrews at this point of the story. We notice first the temporary nature of their stay at Elim. As comfortable as this location was, they knew this was not their final destination. Elim was not the Promised Land. They could not settle here. They had to move on. Further, we notice the fickleness of the attitude of the Hebrews. Either because they were not easily appeased or because they had short memories, the Hebrews would quickly forget the former promises and provisions of God. The moment a hardship arose, they would lose their respect for Moses, and their trust in God would evaporate. They demonstrated this fickleness in this experience.

Instead of trusting God with their future, they longed for the good old days that never were.

As the Hebrews left Elim, they moved southward into the Desert of Sin. The word "sin" does not refer to evil or disobedience toward God but is rather related to the Hebrew word for the bush before which Moses had bowed in awed reverence back in Exodus 3:2. It pictures the rough terrain and scraggly underbrush of the desert.

The terrain was not what bothered the Hebrews, however. The echoes of hunger pain emanating from their stomachs disturbed them. Having been gone from Egypt for about a month, they were running out of food (16:1). When we face difficult circumstances in the present, we often turn for relief either to the past or to the future. The Hebrews chose the former tactic, crying out for what they had left behind in Egypt, which they obviously remembered more glowingly than it had actually been.

In the dialogue that followed between Moses and God, we see that the issue was not a lack of trust in Moses but a lack of trust in God. Therefore, when God met their needs, the supply of their needs would not come from Moses but from God. God promised through Moses that he would provide an abundant supply of food for the people. Eventually God provided both meat and bread.

That very evening a flock of quail landed in the midst of their camp, and the Hebrews were able to seize the birds to provide some meat. The next morning, God provided the strange desert bread that came to be known as "manna." The name for this desert bread came from the initial question of the people when they saw this bread. "What is it?" they asked. "What is it?" translates the Hebrew term *man hu,* a term that was transliterated into "manna" (16:15). The Hebrew people complained that God was not supplying a consistent food source. In response, God provided manna, which would be their primary food every day for the next forty years (16:35)! God met their needs, and then some.

The moment a hardship arose, they would lose their respect for Moses, and their trust in God would evaporate.

God did not just want to meet the needs of the Hebrew people, however. He also wanted to instruct them.

First, God wanted to test them to see whether they would be obedient (16:4). He instructed them to take only enough for one day, assuring them more would come the following day. Too, God instructed them to take a double portion on the sixth day so they would not have to gather the manna on the Sabbath. Many failed this test. Rather than obeying Moses' instructions, they took more than they needed for one day (16:20). Evidently, the Hebrews would need some more lessons on obedience.

Second, God wanted to reveal to them his glory (16:6–7). As the story develops we discover that the Hebrews would need many more instructions before they learned to recognize the full dimensions of God's glory.

At Rephidim on the Sinai Peninsula (17:1–7)

An undisclosed amount of time passed as the Hebrew people wandered around on the Sinai Peninsula. Finally, they arrived at Rephidim, near Mount Sinai. Once again complaints arose, because the people were thirsty. Understandably, with such a large flock of people wandering through the desert, water would be a problem. Again the need erupted into a complaint against Moses and against God. The people's complaint reflected a doubt about God's adequacy to provide for their needs.

Moses responded to their complaints with despair. God, on the other hand, simply responded with a solution. Instructing Moses to strike a certain rock out of which the water would come, God solved the dilemma. Surprisingly, Moses gave two names to the place, one that described the contention of the people (Meribah) and the other that reflected the fact that the people were testing God by their complaints (Massah). Once again, God proved to be sufficient to meet the needs of his people.

In the Battle Against the Amalekites (17:8–16)

The troubles were not over for the recently freed slaves. The Amalekites, a desert tribe bent on their destruction, suddenly confronted them. The Amalekites were an ancient nomadic people who dwelt mainly in the Negev, the desert region to the south of Judea.

Again, God prevailed in a combination of divine intervention and human effort. God used four individuals to accomplish the defeat of the Amalekites. Joshua was the field general who led the troops into battle. Moses inspired the troops as he held his hands up before the Hebrews to signal the blessing of God on their efforts. Aaron and Hur were the support people who held up Moses' hands until the battle was won.

God met their needs, and then some.

Notice two intriguing elements in this story. For one thing, the biblical text mentions Joshua for the first time. The young man was to play a significant part in the Hebrew's unfolding saga (17:9). In addition, the biblical text calls attention to a scroll on which Moses is ordered to write an account of this battle (17:14). What is this book? Some suggest that this is the Book of Jashar, a book that no longer exists but that is quoted from time to time in the Old Testament (Joshua 10:13; 2 Samuel 1:18).

Their Characteristics and Ours

We often boldly affirm, *God is always the same; God does not change from generation to generation.* That is certainly true. But we could accurately affirm also, *Humanity is always the same; we do not change from generation to generation.* Perhaps a good way to apply this lesson is simply to identify the characteristics of the Hebrews as they wandered in the wilderness that also appear in God's children today.

Others connect this scroll with the Book of the Wars of the Lord, referred to in Numbers 21:14. Or perhaps this is an early reference to the writing that eventually became our Old Testament.

To commemorate this victory, Moses constructed an altar to the Lord and dedicated the altar to "the LORD is my Banner" (Exod. 17:15). As a rallying point for armies as they went into battle, a banner was held high to identify and inspire the troops. For Israel, God would be their banner. As God had led to victory over the Amalekites, God would lead Israel from victory to victory as he accomplished his purpose.

Implications for Today

These experiences of the Hebrews in the wilderness teach us some lessons about ourselves. For one thing, like the Hebrews, we often long for the good old days. Somehow, with the passing of time, we tend to glamorize past experiences and forget the difficulties we encountered during those past experiences. As the old saying states, "Things aren't like they used to be, but then, they never were."

> *Instead of being thankful for what we have, we complain about what we don't have.*

In addition, like the Hebrews, we are often unwilling to sacrifice our personal desires for the good of the group. Self-centeredness leads to selfishness. Not necessarily with our words but often with our actions we declare, *As long as my needs and the needs of my family are taken care of, I don't care about anyone else.*

Further, like the Hebrews, we often focus on the negative instead of the positive. Instead of being thankful for what we have, we complain about what we don't have. The resulting ingratitude often forces words of complaint from our lips instead of words of thanksgiving.

This experience of the Hebrews in the wilderness also teaches some lessons about God. For one thing, like the Hebrews, we discover that God's timing is not always our timing. We say to God, *Give us what we want—right now.* But many times, God responds, *I will give you what you need—at the right time.*

In addition, like the Hebrews, we discover that God does not always answer our prayers in the way we expect. The Bible is filled with experiences where God's answer came, but in a different form than the request. God's word to Elijah in a "gentle whisper" (1 Kings 19:12), and God's decision to strengthen Paul, not by removing his thorn but by leaving it in his life (2 Corinthians 12:8–9), are but two examples.

Moreover, like the Hebrews, we discover that God's provisions are sufficient. In God's time, and in God's way, God will supply all our needs (Philippians 4:19).

QUESTIONS

1. What are some evidences of self-centeredness in the church today?

2. What are some evidences of ingratitude in the church today?

3. Why do we so often look at the context of our lives from a negative perspective instead of evaluating it from a positive perspective?

4. Can you think of a time in your life when God revealed his sufficiency to meet your need?

5. Can you think of someone in your church who has reflected a strong and consistent faith in the midst of difficult times?

6. When you offer thanksgiving to God, what are some of the things for which you are thankful?

Guidance for Covenant Living

Unit three treats some of the most exciting passages of Scripture in the Old Testament. After the dramatic occurrence of thunder, lightning, trumpet blasts, and smoke descending onto Mount Sinai, the people heard God's instructions for living—which we call the Ten Commandments. This passage is the foundation of Hebrew society. Likewise, these same commandments are the foundation of many laws within American society.

Then, our study moves into the practical applications and implications of the Ten Commandments—particularly, our relationship with our neighbors. Specific and detailed laws cover the treatment of foreigners; prohibitions against thievery, violence, kidnapping, and the abuse of people and animals; and words of caution about the treatment of the poor and widows. Again, this sense of justice and fairness undergirds our own country.

The principles revealed in these few chapters of Scripture are pivotal in human spiritual development. Even non-believers see the importance and practicality of respecting property rights; the importance of respectful children; the destructive power of adultery; the obvious wrongness of murder, stealing, and lying; and the resulting wickedness that comes from coveting. While God's natural revelation to pagan societies is never as clear as that which we receive through Scripture, such revelation is still adequate to teach a sense of right and wrong about many important matters in human relationships.

Unit three, "Guidance for Covenant Living," deals with background Scripture passages from Exodus 19 through Exodus 24. The unit begins with a lesson on God's making the covenant with the Israelites as recorded in Exodus 19. It continues with two lessons on the Ten Commandments in Exodus 20. Lesson eight, "Treat God Like This," is a study of the first four commandments. Lesson nine, "Treat

People Like This," focuses on the fifth through the tenth commandments. Lesson ten is about the detailed laws often called the covenant code or "Book of the Covenant" (24:7).[1]

UNIT THREE, GUIDANCE FOR COVENANT LIVING

Lesson 7	Wonderful Offer, Serious Demand	Exodus 19:1–12
Lesson 8	Treat God Like This	Exodus 20:1–11
Lesson 9	Treat People Like This	Exodus 20:12–17
Lesson 10	The Nitty-Gritty of Covenant Living	Exodus 21:12–17, 22–27; 22:21—23:11

NOTES

1. Unless otherwise indicated, all Scripture quotations in this unit of study are from the New International Version.

Focal Text

Exodus 19:1–12

Background

Exodus 19

Main Idea

Relationship with God
is initiated by God's
grace but depends on
our response to God.

Question to Explore

How do we presume
on God?

Study Aim

To describe the relationship with
God depicted in this passage and
identify implications for my life

Study and Action Emphases

- Affirm the Bible as our authoritative guide
  for life and ministry
- Share the gospel with all people
- Develop a growing, vibrant faith

LESSON SEVEN

Wonderful Offer, Serious Demand

Quick Read

God's covenant with his people is conditional.
Although God loves all without condition, God
keeps his covenant with us based on our proper
response to him.

Who is the most important person on earth you have ever met? Meeting a celebrity, important political figure, famous author, significant hero, or well-known athlete is always exciting. Butterflies and nervousness accompany such a meeting. We usually feel unworthy or small in a famous personality's presence. After all, they are "somebody," and we are unknown beyond our immediate circle of friends and family.

In Exodus 19, Israel came to the mountain of God—Mount Sinai. With the help of God, Moses had led the people out of Egypt to the very mountain where he had met God for the first time (Exodus 3:1–6; see Deuteronomy 5:2). Now, it was time to meet their God. Lightning, thunder, a thick cloud of smoke settling on the mountaintop, and the sound of a very loud trumpet blast intensified the drama. The Scripture adds, "Everyone in the camp trembled" (Exod. 19:16). The situation was very frightening.

One of the most impressive scenes in Exodus is spoken of in 19:17—"Then Moses led the people out of the camp to meet with God, and they stood at the foot of the mountain." Again, the Scripture tells us that smoke billowed up from the mountain and the whole mountain shook violently. The trumpet blast grew louder and louder. When Moses spoke, the voice of God answered him.

The scene must have been awe-inspiring. Later, in Exodus 20:18–19, the people were so terrified that they begged Moses not to let God speak to them. Instead, they cried out that only Moses should speak.

God made the covenant with Israel in this background. The importance of this event was and is monumental for all of God's children in faith. God intended for it to be momentous.

Exodus 19:1–12

¹In the third month after the Israelites left Egypt—on the very day—they came to the Desert of Sinai. ²After they set out from Rephidim, they entered the Desert of Sinai, and Israel camped there in the desert in front of the mountain.

³Then Moses went up to God, and the LORD called to him from the mountain and said, "This is what you are to say to the house of Jacob and what you are to tell the people of Israel: ⁴'You yourselves have seen what I did to Egypt, and how I carried you on eagles' wings and brought you to myself. ⁵Now if you obey me fully and keep my covenant, then out of all nations you will be my treasured possession. Although the whole earth is

mine, [6]you will be for me a kingdom of priests and a holy nation.' These are the words you are to speak to the Israelites."

[7]So Moses went back and summoned the elders of the people and set before them all the words the LORD had commanded him to speak. [8]The people all responded together, "We will do everything the LORD has said." So Moses brought their answer back to the LORD.

[9]The LORD said to Moses, "I am going to come to you in a dense cloud, so that the people will hear me speaking with you and will always put their trust in you." Then Moses told the LORD what the people had said.

[10]And the LORD said to Moses, "Go to the people and consecrate them today and tomorrow. Have them wash their clothes [11]and be ready by the third day, because on that day the LORD will come down on Mount Sinai in the sight of all the people. [12]Put limits for the people around the mountain and tell them, 'Be careful that you do not go up the mountain or touch the foot of it. Whoever touches the mountain shall surely be put to death.

God's Covenant Offer (19:1–6)

As Moses ascended the mountain, God called out to Moses. This showed God's eagerness to begin a covenantal relationship with the Israelite people. Surely, Moses had told the people many times what had happened to him on the mountain of God when he saw the burning bush (3:1–6). They, in turn, must have experienced a sense of euphoria as they approached Sinai. To hear the very voice of Yahweh call to Moses as he climbed the foothill of the mountain was an affirmation of Moses' story.

God began the covenant with Israel in a most formal way. He referred to the people as "the house of Jacob" and "the people of Israel." This has the sound of an official designation. Probably, God intended to clarify exactly the people group with which he was willing to enter into a covenantal agreement. The covenant of Exodus 19 would build on the covenant God made with Abraham, Isaac, and Jacob. Yet, it would go further in setting out the conditions of the future relationship God now intended for Israel and himself.

Next, God reminded the Hebrews that he considered them his "treasured possession" (19:5). All of us have many possessions. However, some of our possessions are more valuable than others. Many factors go into assessing the worth of some object or person. It may be that something is valuable because of how much it cost. The value is often connected to some sentimental reason. We assess worth based on love. Others might not love our children, but we do. They have immense worth to us.

God loved the Hebrews. This love is not explainable. Love is often illogical. It is amazing that God loves us. Even while we were still sinners, God sent his Son to die for our sins (see Romans 5:8). We have value to God based on God's love for us. He found Israel to be his treasured possession and does the same with us today. Today's Christian is God's treasured possession.

God repeated to the people and to Moses the fact of his loving care that had liberated the Hebrews from captivity in Egypt and had brought them into his presence at Sinai. In Exodus 19:4, Yahweh summarized in one sentence their miraculous deliverance and miracle-filled journey.

Who is the most important person on earth you have ever met?

No generation should ever forget the divine and miraculous providence of God. Our own country is obviously blessed by God. We must never forget the miraculous intervention of God in our nation's birth and history. God has been more than good to America. We cannot forget that. Some may attribute America's greatness to human ingenuity. We know it is God's blessing that has preserved us and made us great.

The word "covenant" (19:5) has lost much of its meaning in modern society. A covenant, though, is a binding, formal agreement between two parties. A covenant is similar to our use of the word *contract*. Yet, the word

Mount Sinai

Strangely, we have no certain knowledge of the exact location of Mount Sinai. Although the Sinaitic Peninsula is easily identifiable, the exact mountain known in Scripture as both Mount Horeb and Mount Sinai is lost to us. Elijah knew the mountain (1 Kings 19:8). Several sites for Mount Sinai have been identified through the centuries. Since the sixth century A.D., Jebel Musa has been identified as Mount Sinai (see cover photo). Several other possible sites in the region have been identified as Mount Sinai.

God, in his providence, has kept the location a secret. No doubt some would worship the mountain instead of the God who made a covenant with his people on the mountain. God is greater than mountains, temples, or holy lands. Whereas geographic holy sites are interesting, they are not more important than any place where one meets God. The Ten Commandments forbid worshiping or venerating anything other than God.

"covenant" carries the thought of a more personal agreement than that of a contract. Both parties have responsibilities in a standard covenant. The agreement is conditional. If one party keeps its part of the contract but the other does not, the agreement is in jeopardy. Unless the offending party returns to the original agreement, the covenant voids itself. No agreement works where only one party does all the agreed-upon parts.

The "covenant" God made with Israel thus has an "if" clause in it (19:5). The word "if" indicates a conditional sentence. The covenant is dependent on Israel's obedience to God's revealed law. "If you obey me fully and keep my covenant" is the key to God's promise to make the house of Jacob a treasured possession. Out of all the nations on earth God could have

> *It is amazing that God loves us.*

chosen, God chose little and insignificant Israel. Only God knows why God chose Israel instead of Egypt or Mesopotamia or some other great nation. Only God knows why God chose Abraham, Isaac, or Jacob. God easily could have chosen others. We call this God's providential wisdom. It remains an unexplainable mystery.

Not only did God choose Israel, but God also intended to make them into "a kingdom of priests and a holy nation" (19:6). A "priest" is a representative of God to people and a representative of people to God. God intended this not only for the Levites—the tribe that produced Israel's priests—but for every tribe. Israel's purpose was to be God's witness to the world. They were supposed to be his missionaries. They were supposed to tell all nations about God. They were supposed to represent the true God to all peoples.

The prophet Isaiah echoed this theme as a reminder to the people of his day. Isaiah stated (Isa. 61:6), "And you will be called priests of the LORD, you will be named ministers of our God. . . ." The Apostle Peter picked up the same idea in 1 Peter 2:9, saying, "But you are a chosen people, a royal priesthood, a holy nation, a people belonging to God, that you may declare the praises of him who called you out of darkness into his wonderful light."

God really intends for God's people—whether under the Old Testament covenant or the New Testament covenant—to act and behave like priests. We should accept a collective duty to be priests, as well as an individual duty to be a priest of God to all people with whom we come into contact.

What a magnificent privilege and honor it was for Israel to know that God had chosen them from among all the people groups on earth

(Exod. 19:6). Yet we know that Israel misinterpreted God's choice. Instead of becoming God's kingdom of priests, they became puffed up and had feelings of superiority to others. They looked down on other nations and saw God's salvation as exclusively for themselves. They were unconcerned about being missionaries.

What about your church? Is it fulfilling the covenant it has with God? Is your church acting as God's missionary to all people groups? Israel failed to keep God's covenant, and it cost them dearly. Our churches today must not follow the same route of disobedience.

The People's Response (19:7–8)

Moses went back to tell the Israelites what God said to him. Moses explained the covenant God wanted to make with them. Moses summoned the elders. They, in turn, must have told the people because it was not the elders who responded on behalf of the people. Instead, the people replied to God in unison, "We will do everything the LORD has said" (19:8).

Although the people did not hear the specific provisions of the covenant, they fully understood the demand for obedience. Obedience is the mark of a true follower of God. Satan believes there is God. He knows that Jesus was raised from the dead. However, Satan is not obedient to God. Throughout both the Old and New Testaments, God expects a faith that produces obedience.

Today, we are all well aware that Israel did not keep the "if" clause of the covenant. However, we also know that people cannot be fully and always obedient. We must ask ourselves, did God expect total and complete obedience? God never says anywhere that it is okay to sin or that we are *just human*. God does expect consistency in godly living, a sincere effort to act obediently, and repentance when one does sin. As a minister, I am never surprised that a Christian sins. I am surprised, however, when Christians who sin do not seek forgiveness and repentance.

God is holy and unlike any other.

Israel's sin was that they would abandon God's covenant, become lost in a multitude of sins that violated the covenant, and never feel they had done anything wrong. They became blind to their own sin and became used to a sinful lifestyle without a conscience, deliberately presuming on

God's Awesome Presence

God did not want the people to presume on his mercy. God is holy and separate from humankind. He has awesomeness about himself that we must never take for granted.

No person ever saw God face to face until Jesus (John 1:14, 18). Prior to the birth of Jesus, God stated in Exodus 33:20, "But . . . you cannot see my face, for no one may see me and live." Jacob was wrong when he stated that he had seen the face of God and lived through it (Gen. 32:30). In Jacob's mysterious experience, he saw a toned-down vision of God. All others in Scripture who found themselves in the very presence of holy God fell on their faces before him (see Ezekiel 1:25–28; Revelation 1:17) or covered their faces with a cloak (1 Kings 19:11–13).

We should be careful how we come before God in worship. He is still holy, and an attitude of reverence would befit any meeting with God.

God's good nature. Some must have felt that God did not care whether they sinned and broke the covenant. Or, since they had broken the covenant and nothing had happened, perhaps they assumed God was not going to do anything about their sinfulness. Nevertheless, at this point in Israel's history, the people agreed to God's terms for a covenant.

The Preparation of God's People (19:9–12)

When Moses took the answer of the people back to Yahweh, God explained the procedure for the upcoming meeting between God, Moses, and the people. God intended to speak to Moses from a dense cloud. The people would hear the voice of God speaking to Moses, but they would not see God himself.

> *God really intends for God's people . . . to act and behave like priests.*

The presence of the cloud was not new to the people. They traveled to Sinai with the leadership of the cloud by day and a pillar of fire by night (13:22). Yet, God wanted it clearly understood that Moses was to be the intermediary. Yahweh wanted the people to respect the role of Moses and put their confidence in Moses' leadership.

However, before the meeting could commence, God required that the people consecrate themselves before God. This consecration required the people to wash their clothes. This was to be an outward symbol of the inner cleansing each person was to make. Boundaries were set in place around the foot of the mountain. No one was to set foot on the mountain, except Moses.

God wanted to stress his holiness and the importance of this great moment in the history of humankind. God is holy and unlike any other. God is expecting respect. The mount could not be touched, and it burned with flame and smoke. What a magnificent display of God's awesomeness!

. . . Let us approach God's throne of grace with reverence and not presumption and arrogance.

We must never presume on the wonderful gift given to us through the blood of Jesus. We can enter the very throne room of God to speak with the Creator of the universe. Not only that, but also God welcomes our coming because our sins are blotted out by Christ's work on the cross and Christ's subsequent resurrection.

Therefore, let us approach God's throne of grace with reverence and not presumption and arrogance. Only by God's grace can we stand before God. Although Jesus calls us "friends" (John 15:15), God is still God, and we are but human beings.

QUESTIONS

1. Have you ever thought about how it would be actually to meet God?

2. What kind of personal preparation would you make if you could meet God here on earth?

3. Do you consider yourself a "priest of God"? Why?

4. Do you consider yourself God's "treasured possession"? Why?

5. Does God have an "if" clause in God's covenant with you?

6. How well do you keep your part of your covenant with God? If you are not doing well, what do you think you ought to do?

Focal Text

Exodus 20:1–11

Background

Exodus 20:1–11

Main Idea

Give God your complete loyalty and worship.

Question to Explore

What place does God have in a life like yours?

Study Aim

To explain the first four commandments and identify implications for my life

Study and Action Emphases

- Affirm the Bible as our authoritative guide for life and ministry
- Develop a growing, vibrant faith

LESSON EIGHT

Treat God Like This

Quick Read

The first four commandments summarize a proper relationship between God and humankind. Each commandment calls for total commitment and respect to Yahweh only.

When I was leaving for college, my father took me aside for some last-minute advice. I remember it until this day. He was a very godly, dedicated Christian. He was a deacon and was the son of a Baptist preacher. He said to me, "Son, I want you to try to keep the Ten Commandments as you start out on your own in life. I have found I was happiest when I kept them and was unhappiest when I broke them." My father's advice has been very true in my life.

God did not give us the Ten Commandments to keep us from enjoying life. God gave them to us so that we would relate properly to God and to one another. Rather than being restrictive, the commandments free us to live our lives in joy and happiness.

I believe in the absolute truth of the Ten Commandments. I do not believe in the absolute truth of someone's interpretation as to what they must mean in everyone else's life. The commandments are both specific enough, as well as general enough, to allow for godly people to apply them variously in their individual lives. This does not mean that bizarre or perverted interpretations are tolerated. It means that "Thou shalt not kill" (Exodus 20:13, KJV) is variously understood by equally committed Christian believers. For instance, one may take it literally and oppose every form of killing another human. Other equally dedicated Christians might believe in some form of capital punishment, some cases of abortion, or a need for war. Christianity has never been in full agreement on this particular commandment. It will be discussed more fully in next week's lesson. It only serves here as an illustration of the diversity of Christian belief on the various commandments.

The Ten Commandments are variously numbered by the major Judeo-Christian groups. (See the sidebar on "The Ten Commandments.") Regardless of how one numbers the content of the commandments (20:2–17), none of the holy text is omitted.

Another account of the giving of the Ten Commandments is in Deuteronomy 5:1–22. There are slight differences in the two accounts, but not substantive differences. For instance, compare the fourth commandment in Exodus 20:8–11 with Deuteronomy 5:12–14. The reason for observing the Sabbath day differs. Rather than seeing the two readings as contradictory, it is better to see them as complementary. That is, there are two reasons for observing the Sabbath day. The two do not contradict each other. The Exodus account gives one reason for observing the Sabbath, and the Deuteronomy reading gives a second reason to observe the Sabbath.

Exodus 20:1–11

[1] And God spoke all these words:

[2] "I am the Lord your God, who brought you out of Egypt, out of the land of slavery.

[3] "You shall have no other gods before me.

[4] "You shall not make for yourself an idol in the form of anything in heaven above or on the earth beneath or in the waters below. [5] You shall not bow down to them or worship them; for I, the Lord your God, am a jealous God, punishing the children for the sin of the fathers to the third and fourth generation of those who hate me, [6] but showing love to a thousand generations of those who love me and keep my commandments.

[7] "You shall not misuse the name of the Lord your God, for the Lord will not hold anyone guiltless who misuses his name.

[8] "Remember the Sabbath day by keeping it holy. [9] Six days you shall labor and do all your work, [10] but the seventh day is a Sabbath to the Lord your God. On it you shall not do any work, neither you, nor your son or daughter, nor your manservant or maidservant, nor your animals, nor the alien within your gates. [11] For in six days the Lord made the heavens and the earth, the sea, and all that is in them, but he rested on the seventh day. Therefore the Lord blessed the Sabbath day and made it holy.

The First Commandment (20:2–3)

God explained the basis for requiring these commandments. God had delivered the Israelites from their bondage in Egypt. God wanted it to be clear who was commanding these commandments. It was not Moses. It was not even an angelic being. Instead, it was the very God who had delivered them and brought them to this holy mountain.

God used his distinctive, revealed name—"Yahweh." A literal reading of 20:1–2a reads, "And *Elohim* spoke all these words. I am *Yahweh* your *Elohim*." One can easily see that *Elohim* is a generic term for God or any god. It is like our English word *god*. It appears often in Scripture and can refer to false gods. However, *Yahweh* is the revealed name for God, which God gave to Moses from the burning bush (Exod. 3). This *Yahweh* is the true and only God.

God pointed to his divine deliverance in bringing the Israelites out of Egypt. God was exercising his authority and right to be Israel's one true

God. He did not base his authority on the fact that he is the Creator but based it on his divine mercy and ability to deliver his people. He sought obedience based on one's love and appreciation of God, rather than on God's awesome power that causes fear. God is still seeking believers who serve him out of love and devotion rather than a fear of going to hell. God prefers a loving devotion from God's people.

> God prefers a loving devotion from God's people.

God made it clear in the first commandment that he would tolerate no other gods (*Elohim*). The phrase "before me" literally means *before my face*. God's followers are to have nothing that stands in the way of God's face or presence. God is very demanding in this matter. God knows human nature. Humankind is very capable of giving Yahweh second, third, fourth, or even no place at all. Humanity appears to be very susceptible to displacing God or moving him behind other gods. Families, occupation, hobbies, material goods, honors, education, sports, personal goals, along with many other factors can be made first in our lives. The ancients had similar distractions. Yahweh wants first loyalty, first respect, first devotion, and first place. Our ultimate loyalty is to God alone. Jesus said, "Love the Lord your God with all your heart and with all your soul and with all your mind and with all your strength" (Mark 12:30).

God made the first commandment an individual responsibility. He said literally, "There is not to be to you [singular] other gods before my face" (Exod. 20:3). Notice the bracketed word. "You" is singular. No individual is to have any other gods before God. It is not just a national or group responsibility, but rather it is an individual one. The keeping of this commandment is personalized to each human being.

> I believe in the absolute truth of the Ten Commandments. I do not believe in the absolute truth of someone's interpretation as to what they must mean in everyone else's life.

Although there really are no other gods, Yahweh was not specifically teaching monotheism in this commandment. That is taught in other Scriptures. God recognizes that other religions claim that they too have gods. However, Yahweh was commanding that you must not mix the true God revealed in Yahweh with the worship or devotion to other religions and their gods. Judaism and Christianity are both exclusive religions. Even though we live in a world that cries out against exclusiveness, Yahweh demands exclusive recognition of himself as the only God. He will tolerate no recognition of any other god or religion.

The Second Commandment (20:4–6)

As the first commandment demands the recognition of the one true God, the second forbids erecting any image purporting to be a representation of Yahweh. No graven image would ever be sufficient to capture the majesty and glory of Almighty God. No artist, sculptor, silversmith, gold artisan, iron maker, woodcrafter, stonemason, or any other artisan could ever render an image of the Creator and God of the universe.

Nevertheless, humankind tries to do just that. Pagans have misunderstood the revelation of God in nature. Instead of worshiping the One who made the ox, cat, bird, sun, moon, human, tree, water, fire, thunder, and lightning (and the list could include anything in the physical universe), we create an image of the object and mistakenly worship it. Without regard for this explicit prohibition against making images for worship, people invariably fall into this trap.

Even the Israelites forgot this teaching on many occasions. Some had household gods in image form that they regularly worshiped. Others openly participated in idol worship and adopted pagan rituals and pagan morality. Some Old Testament kings even sacrificed their own children to pagan deities.

We often shrink in horror at such activity, while forgetting our own idol worship. God has revealed himself to us through his Son, Jesus. Christians need no other affirmation of faith.

For many years, Baptists refused to place a cross on their steeples or anywhere inside the church. Today, we view such items as mere symbols of our faith. Whereas a "pulpit" Bible may appear on the Lord's Supper table in many Baptist churches, no one bows down to it or worships it. The Bible is the word of God. The Bible is not God himself. Whereas we have deep respect for the Bible, we do not treat it as a magic talisman or charm to ward off evil and protect us from harm. The God of whom the Bible speaks protects us.

We must be vigilant to explain to children that portraits of Christ are merely an artist's representation of how Jesus might have looked. Portraits are not adequate pictures of the true Christ.

The Third Commandment (20:7)

Usually this commandment has been interpreted as referring to not using God's name in connection with a swear word or a vulgarity. While this commandment certainly means that, it really means much more than just that.

A better translation of the commandment would read, "Do not take the Lord your God's name *lightly*." For Hebrews, the use of God's name meant to be able to call on God for action. There is power in God's name. To use God's name for any purpose other than the most respectable and noble reasons is to misuse God's name. It is blasphemy to use God's name for common or vulgar reasons unrelated to the holiness of God's being.

God did not give us the Ten Commandments to keep us from enjoying life.

One can blaspheme the name of God without using obscenities or swear words. Flippant and casual expressions can demean the nature of God's holy name. One must be very careful in a so-called "harmless joke." God certainly must have a sense of humor and would gladly enjoy a joyous occasion. However, some banter God's name about so freely that it loses its holiness and distinctiveness. A common phrase heard often is "Oh, my God!" Usually the person is expressing simple surprise and nothing more. The words are empty. The phrase is not a religious expression or even a prayer for divine help, which it could be if used properly. Instead, it is uttered as an expletive.

Yahweh wants first loyalty, first respect, first devotion, and first place.

Of course, God's name can be used wrongly to utter an obscenity. I have often marveled that no other deity has been used this way—at least not in my hearing. I do not hear people using the name of Buddha, Allah, or Hare Krishna in such a vulgar fashion. The reason people—both unbelievers and believers—use God's name or Jesus' name is because these are powerful names. "God Almighty" is a powerful swear word. "Buddha Almighty" does not seem to carry the same force.

Christians must never treat God's name lightly. The Jews came to a place where they refused to utter the name *Yahweh*. This is still the case in Judaism today. In the holy text where the name *Yahweh* appears, modern Judaism still substitutes the word *Adonai*, which means *Lord*. Their reasoning is based on this commandment. Judaism fears being guilty of ever taking God's name lightly, and so Jews take care not to say God's name at all.

While Baptists believe that God's name is holy, we do say it reverently. It is not used in our prayers as vain repetition. Such a use cheapens the majesty of God's name. His name is not a "filler" in our prayers. We speak it only because we are addressing the God of the universe. Jesus is our Lord and God. His name is indeed wonderful.

The Fourth Commandment (20:8–11)

The first time the word "Sabbath" is used in Scripture is found in Exodus 16:23. In giving instructions on how and when to gather manna, Moses made provision for gathering an extra amount only on the day before the Sabbath or seventh day. Even in Exodus 16:23, the reason Moses gave for preparing more was because the Sabbath was to be a holy day—a day of rest.

The Ten Commandments

Sometimes people are unaware that the listing or numbering of the Ten Commandments is not the same for Judaism, Roman Catholicism, Lutherans, and other Protestants. In Judaism, the first commandment is 20:2. The second is 20:3–6, and then the numbering (20:7–17) is the same as in Protestantism. Among Roman Catholics and Lutherans, the first commandment is 20:2–6; the second commandment is 20:7; the third is 20:8–11; the fourth through eighth are the same as for other Protestants and Jews (20:12–16); the ninth is 20:17a; and the tenth is 20:17b. Among Protestants (except Lutherans) the first is 20:2–3; the second is 20:4–6; the third is 20:7; the fourth is 20:8–11; and the fifth through tenth are the same as for Judaism (20:12–17).[1]

Whereas there is no omission of any of the biblical text, the numbering differs. Many times a group will abbreviate a longer passage and not give the whole text in its abbreviation. For instance, "Remember the Sabbath day by keeping it holy" does not include in the abbreviation all of the text relating to the Sabbath day. The full text of this commandment is 20:8–11. The abbreviation serves well to aid in remembering easily the Ten Commandments. Yet, to fully understand the commandment, one must read the full text to derive God's teaching. In light of the variety of ways of numbering the Ten Commandments, one who wants to post them must first answer the question, *Which rendering of the commandments do we post?*

According to this commandment, the Hebrews were to cease all work on the Sabbath. Everyone within the household was to cease all work. Even a Gentile visitor or unbeliever was not to work on the Sabbath if the person was visiting in the home of an Israelite.

The reason God gave for the cessation of work on the Sabbath was that God rested from creation on the seventh day. Thus, the Sabbath observes God's rest in creation. Humankind is also supposed to pause once every seven days for rest.

In Deuteronomy 5:15, God tied the rest of maidservants and menservants within the Hebrew home to the fact that the Hebrews themselves were at one time bondslaves in Egypt. The Israelites were to show the same consideration for their own servants as they themselves enjoyed.

Notice that God did not command worship in this passage, and neither did God command worship on the Sabbath anywhere in Scripture. The Scripture does show the Jews worshiping on the Sabbath, but there is no command. The command is that the day will be "holy" (Exod. 20:11). The word "holy" means *separate* and *distinct*. The Sabbath is not to be like any other day.

As the first commandment demands the recognition of the one true God, the second forbids erecting any image purporting to be a representation of Yahweh.

There certainly is no prohibition or encouragement in Scripture to not worship God on the Sabbath. In reality, it is one of the best times to pause and listen to God and praise God's name in corporate worship. Furthermore, Scripture cautions believers not to quit assembling for worship (Hebrews 10:25).

Another important point for our day needs some discussion. "Rest" may be variously interpreted. It does not always mean a nap or just sitting on the couch watching television. Rest takes many forms. The admonition of this passage is to "rest" from your labor. One person's rest is another person's labor and vice versa.

It is very difficult to draw up a list of prohibited practices and acceptable practices. The Jews did this. They had thirty-nine different laws to interpret what was and what was not acceptable. Baptists have also been guilty of such lists. As a child I was prohibited from going to a movie theater on Sunday. Even so, with the advent of television, my stern father would rush the family home on Sunday evenings so he could see "Sunday Night at the Movies." Too, there is nothing in Scripture that states the number of worship services in which one should participate on the Sabbath. Once when my brother and I were children, we were playing sandlot football on a Sunday afternoon. We went to church morning and evening. Yet, a neighbor who attended our church came out and reprimanded all of us for playing ball on the Sabbath. The game ended abruptly, but my mother told my brother and me not to believe the neighbor. In Mom's opinion, it was okay to have fun on the Christian Sabbath as long as we also used the day to worship God. I have remembered my mom's teaching all these years.

Christians must never treat God's name lightly.

Today, however, some see Sunday as only a day to play. They ignore God, worship, missions, hymn singing, offerings, Bible teaching, and good preaching every week. This is not right. God commanded that the seventh day was to be holy. To do less than to make it holy is to violate this commandment.

QUESTIONS

1. Are you keeping the first four commandments?

2. What are some ways in which people today are worshiping other gods or worshiping idols?

3. What do you believe are acceptable ways to use God's name? Do you disagree with the writer on the illustrations he gives of the misuse of God's name today?

4. Do you know of a church that has rules and regulations regarding what they believe to be proper Christian behavior on the Christian Sabbath?

5. Why do most Christians consider Sunday as their Sabbath to the Lord?

NOTES

1. Page H. Kelley, *Exodus: Called for Redemptive Mission* (Nashville, Tennessee: Convention Press, 1977), 110.

Focal Text

Exodus 20:12–17

Background

Exodus 20:12–17

Main Idea

Respect your fellow human beings and their rights.

Question to Explore

How is belief in God related to how we treat our fellow human beings?

Study Aim

To explain the final six commandments and state implications for my life

Study and Action Emphases

- Affirm the Bible as our authoritative guide for life and ministry
- Develop a growing, vibrant faith
- Include all God's family in decision-making and service
- Value all people as created in the image of God
- Encourage healthy families
- Obey and serve Jesus by meeting physical, spiritual, and emotional needs

LESSON NINE

Treat People Like This

Quick Read

Commandments five through ten show us how God expects us to relate to our family and to people around us. These commandments are guidelines for happy living with our family and other people.

Jesus was asked which was the greatest of all the commandments. He answered, "'Love the Lord your God with all your heart and with all your soul and with all your mind and with all your strength.' The second is this: 'Love your neighbor as yourself.' There is no commandment greater than these" (Mark 12:30–31).

It is easy to see that Jesus summarized the entire Ten Commandments into these two statements. Notice that the first summarizes commandments one through four. The second statement summarizes commandments five through ten. The entire law and prophets hinge on these two summaries. It is well to know each of the commandments from memory. However, when memory fails us, we can rely on this digest of the Ten Commandments.

Commandments five through ten were obligations of members of the believing community to one another. Not only are these six commandments an obligation, but they are also a larger part of our agreement with God. The first four are a basis for the last six. We must relate first and properly to God. Then, we have a divine responsibility to our neighbors. One cannot love God and hate one's neighbor (see 1 John 4:20–21). The two cannot be separated. These last six commandments are still commandments. The true Christian will seek the aid of the Holy Spirit to keep each of them.

Exodus 20:12–17

[12]"Honor your father and your mother, so that you may live long in the land the Lord your God is giving you.

[13]"You shall not murder.

[14]"You shall not commit adultery.

[15]"You shall not steal.

[16]"You shall not give false testimony against your neighbor.

[17]"You shall not covet your neighbor's house. You shall not covet your neighbor's wife, or his manservant or maidservant, his ox or donkey, or anything that belongs to your neighbor."

The Fifth Commandment (20:12)

The commandment begins by calling on us to honor father and mother. The key word in this sentence is "honor." It carries several meanings in

Hebrew, all of which are somewhat related. It can mean *prize highly, care for, show respect for, be heavy,* or *give weight to.* Any one of these definitions would be appropriate. However, "honor" is still the best of all since it really does encompass each of these others.

Honor for parents is a godly act. Disrespect for parents is ungodly. It is quite true that some parents are not worthy of respect. Sometimes a parent's behavior toward the children is neglectful, self-centered, manipulative, and abusive. Such parents are not worthy of the title *parent.*

> *We must relate first and properly to God. Then, we have a divine responsibility to our neighbors.*

Parents are supposed to be teachers and examples to their children. Parents should reflect the glory of God in their lives. In turn, children should grow up under the loving care of such parents and respond with respect and devotion. Children should recognize that parents have more experience with what is right and wrong. Parents have observed the pitfalls of life and should steer the children through the difficulties life presents. Parents are obligated to equip their children with godly values and ethical behavior that will serve them as they grow up and move out into the world.

As a result of such goodness on the part of parents, children should acknowledge the role God has placed on fathers and mothers. Notice that the child is to honor both father and mother equally.

There comes a day in many children's lives when their mom or dad will be dependent on the child. The child must not see this as a burden. It is a natural part of life. It is no more of a burden or chore to care for your parents in their older years than it was for them to care for you during your first eighteen to twenty-one years of life. In the Bible, there was no "Social Security." The only known Social Security was in one's family. Often a

> *Respect and honor your mother and father.*

parent lived in the home with the married child and grandchildren. Such parents received great honor and respect from both the children and the grandchildren. Politeness, courtesy, and respectful conversation are all hallmarks of honoring one's parents.

This is the first commandment with a promise. If one honors father and mother, the Scripture promises a long life on this earth. The reason is simple. Such a person will be a happier person. Science has discovered that happier people tend to live longer than unhappy people. Respect and honor your mother and father. Likewise, moms and dads must be worthy of such honor and respect.

The Sixth Commandment (20:13)

The Hebrew word for murder usually refers to a premeditated or deliberate act of murder. Taking another person's life in any circumstance is serious business. Since we believe that every person is created in the image of God and that God creates every person, premeditated murder is forbidden. It is an attack on God and on God's own creation.

Human life belongs to God and is sacred. At no point in human existence is life not sacred. From conception until one's last breath, all of human life is holy. Consequently, to cause a life to cease is no small matter. There are many ways to take human life: abortion, accident, war, capital punishment, removing life support in a hospital, murder, self defense, suicide, and any number of variations of these listed.

Christians are not in agreement on the matter of taking human life. Capital punishment and abortion are two current hot topics in discussions of Christian ethics. In times past, war has occupied center stage in the debate. During World War II, Southern Baptists adopted a position that recognized conscientious objectors. Although most Baptists supported that war, it was felt that provision needed to be made for those who objected on religious conviction.

Human life belongs to God and is sacred.

The Mosaic law set up a system by which a murderer would receive a fair trial. Cities of refuge were scattered throughout the country (Numbers 35:6–12). A person guilty of murder could flee to one of the six cities and there await trial without fear of being murdered by the victim's family or friends. Furthermore, the Mosaic code required the testimony of two witnesses, preferably three, to establish the truth of an accusation (Deut. 19:15). Finally, the Jews set up an elaborate appeal process. Unfortunately, these safeguards were not always followed honestly. Such was the case in the trial of Jesus.

The lesson to be learned is that the taking of human life is a very serious matter. It should always be a last resort. It should be used through proper authorities and never through one person acting alone, except in the matter of self-defense or accidental, unintended death.

Jesus and the Ten Commandments

The longest teaching on the Ten Commandments (and other portions of the Mosaic law) that Jesus gave is found in the Sermon on the Mount (Matthew 5:21–47). In this sermon, Jesus gave a more in-depth explanation of God's original intention and thoughts behind the commandments. Jesus pointed out that the breaking of the commandments begins in our hearts with our thought process. Jesus removed any hope of innocently saying, *I have never committed murder or adultery.* In light of the teachings in these verses, we all find ourselves guilty of violating God's laws.

Furthermore, Jesus summarized all the Ten Commandments and the law and prophets in Mark 12:29–31. Jesus quoted in these verses from Deuteronomy 6:4–5 and Leviticus 19:18. Loving God and loving our fellow human beings are the essence of godly living for a believer.

A believer's life is a changed life. That life should give evidence of love for God and all humankind. Jesus demonstrated these two principles in his earthly life. He is our perfect example of how to keep the Ten Commandments.

The Seventh Commandment (20:14)

Adultery is a sin against both God and one's marriage partner. The implications of the Hebrew word for adultery can include premarital as well as extra-marital sexual relations. Since we live in a narcissistic society that is bent toward personal rights and freedoms above group rights, our society is guilty of breaking this commandment.

God intended for the family to be a stable human relationship. It is the very first institution established by God, in the marriage of Adam and Eve. God wants a family headed by a husband and wife who genuinely love and respect each other. A husband becomes an example of how a God-fearing man behaves toward his wife and children. He represents the kind of man his sons are to be. Likewise, he represents the kind of man his daughters are to marry. The same is true for the wife. She, too, is to be the same kind of godly example to her sons and daughters. The children deserve a household environment in which they can depend on their parents. The absence of a father or mother is less than God's perfect will.

Adultery attacks the family at its most basic point—trust. An unreliable marriage partner is less than a full partner. Stability is shaken and sometimes irreparably broken. Adultery is almost always premeditated.

Jesus said it begins in the heart as lust (Matthew 5:28). Some people think that adultery is only sexual intercourse. Jesus said it is lust.

Some years ago, when President Jimmy Carter, a Baptist, admitted that he had committed adultery in his heart, television comedians and the national press had a field day. The problem was that those who commented on his admission did not know the Scripture, but President Carter did. Although he was not proud of his lustful thoughts, he was honorable in his confession of his sin. Regardless of one's political feelings about President Carter as a President, any Christian would do well to follow his example in this matter. We need to be ever watchful that our thoughts do not lead us into activity that threatens our sacred marriage vows. Jesus indicated that we should take radical action to remove ourselves from lustful or adulterous situations (Matt. 5:29–30).

The Eighth Commandment (20:15)

Like the prohibitions in commandments six and seven, this commandment is stated in stark terms. Basically, it says, "You shall not steal." At first glance, one might think, *How much interpretation is needed here?* It appears very straightforward.

Yet, stealing is rampant in American life. It is more than just robbing a bank, mugging a person on the street, or burglarizing a home or business. It has at its basic level *greed*. While there is little doubt that this commandment is related to the tenth commandment about coveting, it easily stands on its own merit. The taking of that which is not rightfully yours is a sin against your neighbor and God.

This sin involves white-collar crime as well as ordinary theft. Unfortunately, some executives in America have stolen employee pension plans and bank savings, engaged in price gouging and illegal stock sales or buying methods, and established disproportionate salaries and bonuses. Ordinary employees have failed to give a full day of hard work for a fair wage. Some employees pilfer office supplies or take tools that do not belong to them. Others misrepresent their actual income to the Internal Revenue Service. Some use employee equipment without permission for their own private gain. Some misstate actual costs in medical and insurance claims. Fraud and shoplifting are a serious problem.

Adultery attacks the family at its most basic point—trust.

A Christian needs to make a conscious decision to be honest in business and other human relationships. Integrity should carry over from a church service or Bible study into daily living and ethical relationships. Ministers, deacons, Bible teachers, and ordinary members should guard their honesty. An honest person never has to be shy in expecting a fair wage for hard, honest labor.

The Ninth Commandment (20:16)

Lying is one of the most abominable sins to God. Yet, we often treat it rather lightly on many occasions. Lying is probably the most common of all sins. Everyone at one time or another has lied. However, it receives condemnation in the Ten Commandments. In Proverbs 6:16–19, a list appears that the writer describes as follows: "There are six things which the Lord hates, Yes, seven which are an abomination to Him" (NASB). The NIV uses the word "detestable" instead of "abomination." The King James Version and New Revised Standard Version also use the word "abomination." The implication is that God finds lying utterly repulsive. In Revelation 21:8, one finds another list of sins for which one will be cast into hell. The passage says all liars shall be cast into hell. Consequently, a Christian should take this prohibition more seriously.

Specifically, this commandment prohibits false testimony against one's neighbor. Even with this restriction, it is a terrible sin that touches many lives. Gossip, slander, rumor, and outright lying about a person are forbidden. Nevertheless, some feel compelled to repeat untruths regardless of whether they have been verified. "So-and-so said" should be a red flag to every thinking Christian. The question to be asked is, *Did you see it with your own eyes or hear it with your own ears?* If not, the item is questionable. Already, our study has pointed out that one must have the testimony of two or three eyewitnesses before a statement can be verified. Without such incontrovertible witnesses, a story becomes suspect.

> *Integrity should carry over from a church service or Bible study into daily living and ethical relationships.*

It is too easy to lie. Whatever the motive for the lie, it is a sin against God and against your neighbor. The church should refuse gossip and scorn the gossiper.

The Tenth Commandment (20:17)

The Apostle Paul confessed that this was a sin he understood through the law (Romans 7:7). Although Paul did not actually say he coveted, one might get the impression that he had.

Coveting is the root of many other sins. The prohibition against coveting lists many areas where one might covet wrongly. For instance, do not covet someone's wife (or spouse), manservant, maidservant, ox, donkey, or anything else belonging to someone else. Coveting precedes theft, lying, adultery, and sometimes murder.

Coveting destabilizes society. It attacks basic human rights and puts one at odds with God. Envy and jealousy are the evil twins of coveting. The ownership of property or the relationship one has with a spouse, even a friend, is at risk when coveting is entertained.

Since we live in a society that is obsessed with material things, coveting is a prominent sin. The undisciplined life of wanting something and wanting it now has destroyed many people and relationships. Sometimes we are out of control. We go into deep debt to keep up with friends and neighbors. Sometimes we are motivated by having the latest and greatest. Not willing to wait or save up to purchase an item, we covet a thing so badly that all reason is thrown to the wind. Bad choices result. Many of those bad choices cause grief for both others and us as a final result.

Coveting is the root of many other sins.

The media creates attractive marketing for products. Often unsubstantiated claims are made. Happiness is promised by the mere ownership or possession of some products. The result is a life driven by false gods. We lose perspective. Our values are distorted. Cheating, lying, greed, malice, and unhappiness ensue. Finally, we find ourselves with many things but are still unhappy and unfulfilled.

The life of one who covets will never reach satisfaction. Life is more than the mere possession of a late model car, a modern house with modern appliances, glittering jewelry, name-brand clothing, the best education, top-of-the-line furniture, or up-to-date electronic gadgets. Seeking after and possessing such things may even indicate a shallow view of God's true purpose in life.

There is nothing wrong in admiring beautiful or modern things. However, when such items become the major reason for living the good life, sin results. Coveting a neighbor's possession takes one's attention away from godly pursuits. Jesus cautioned that life is more than clothing, shelter, and fine things (Matt. 6:19–21, 25–33).

A person's treasure should be noble and godly. A person's treasure should never be measured by the number of possessions accumulated. Rather, our greatest treasures should be the life we have lived according to God's purposes.

QUESTIONS

1. Are your parents living? If so, how do you show them "honor"? Specifically, what do you do?

2. What do you think the sixth commandment says about abortion, war, capital punishment, and suicide?

3. How serious a problem is adultery in American society?

4. Do you know of any illustrations in which people steal from one another—other than burglary and robbery?

5. Do you feel that lying is as serious a sin as the other commandments? Does your life demonstrate that you consider it a serious sin?

6. What are some social implications of covetousness?

Focal Text

Exodus 21:12–17,
22–27; 22:21—23:11

Background

Exodus 20:22—24:18

Main Idea

Faithfulness to the
covenant with God
affects the details of
every aspect of life.

Question to Explore

How does following
God affect the details
of your daily life?

Study Aim

To summarize the teachings of the covenant
code and evaluate how they speak to life today

Study and Action Emphases

- Affirm the Bible as our authoritative guide
  for life and ministry
- Develop a growing, vibrant faith
- Include all God's family in decision-making
  and service
- Value all people as created in the image of
  God
- Encourage healthy families
- Obey and serve Jesus by meeting physical,
  spiritual, and emotional needs
- Equip people for servant leadership

LESSON TEN

The Nitty-Gritty of Covenant Living

Quick Read

After understanding the nature of God's covenant
and knowing the commandments of God, one
must use this divine knowledge in a practical way
in everyday life.

Genuine faith acts out its belief in daily living. Very few people read the Bible and stay confused about the will and purpose of God. Someone has said, "It is not what I do not understand in the Bible that bothers me; it is what I do understand that bothers me."

Every serious child of God knows this feeling. We fully understand exactly what God requires or expects, and it is our failure to do what is right that bothers us. Most of us want to understand God's word. In the passage selected for today's study, we have the beginning of how the law of God is to be administered in our lives. This passage is called "the Book of the Covenant" (see Exodus 24:7) or the *covenant code*. The reason is obvious. This body of material involves many aspects of carrying out the covenant God has made with Israel.

The larger context (Exod. 20:22—24:18) begins with guidelines for worship. God expanded the demand of no other gods rivaling his place in worship and specified the preparation of the worship altar. God gave instructions about the proper treatment of slaves, the correct reaction to violent acts against people, and the fair treatment of animals. God expanded the laws to encompass property rights, debt, treatment of Gentiles, and marriage.

Many of the laws appear to be cultural in nature. That is, they are not specific timeless truths and laws but are tied to the culture of that day. On the other hand, even cultural laws have an underlying principle to be observed by modern Christians in their behavior. Putting to death a person who curses his or her father or mother (21:17) is not practiced today by any Christian group of which this writer is aware. However, every group teaches respect and honor for parents. The law is cultural, but the timeless truth behind the law is still relevant in every Christian's life.

Exodus 21:12–17, 22–27

[12]"Anyone who strikes a man and kills him shall surely be put to death. [13]However, if he does not do it intentionally, but God lets it happen, he is to flee to a place I will designate. [14]But if a man schemes and kills another man deliberately, take him away from my altar and put him to death.

[15]"Anyone who attacks his father or his mother must be put to death.

[16]"Anyone who kidnaps another and either sells him or still has him when he is caught must be put to death.

[17]"Anyone who curses his father or mother must be put to death.

²²"If men who are fighting hit a pregnant woman and she gives birth prematurely but there is no serious injury, the offender must be fined whatever the woman's husband demands and the court allows. ²³But if there is serious injury, you are to take life for life, ²⁴eye for eye, tooth for tooth, hand for hand, foot for foot, ²⁵burn for burn, wound for wound, bruise for bruise.

²⁶"If a man hits a manservant or maidservant in the eye and destroys it, he must let the servant go free to compensate for the eye. ²⁷And if he knocks out the tooth of a manservant or maidservant, he must let the servant go free to compensate for the tooth.

Exodus 22:21–31

²¹"Do not mistreat an alien or oppress him, for you were aliens in Egypt.

²²"Do not take advantage of a widow or an orphan. ²³If you do and they cry out to me, I will certainly hear their cry. ²⁴My anger will be aroused, and I will kill you with the sword; your wives will become widows and your children fatherless.

²⁵"If you lend money to one of my people among you who is needy, do not be like a moneylender; charge him no interest. ²⁶If you take your neighbor's cloak as a pledge, return it to him by sunset, ²⁷because his cloak is the only covering he has for his body. What else will he sleep in? When he cries out to me, I will hear, for I am compassionate.

²⁸"Do not blaspheme God or curse the ruler of your people.

²⁹"Do not hold back offerings from your granaries or your vats.

"You must give me the firstborn of your sons. ³⁰Do the same with your cattle and your sheep. Let them stay with their mothers for seven days, but give them to me on the eighth day.

³¹"You are to be my holy people. So do not eat the meat of an animal torn by wild beasts; throw it to the dogs.

Exodus 23:1–11

¹"Do not spread false reports. Do not help a wicked man by being a malicious witness.

²"Do not follow the crowd in doing wrong. When you give testimony in a lawsuit, do not pervert justice by siding with the crowd, ³and do not show favoritism to a poor man in his lawsuit.

⁴"If you come across your enemy's ox or donkey wandering off, be sure to take it back to him. ⁵If you see the donkey of someone who hates you fallen down under its load, do not leave it there; be sure you help him with it.

⁶"Do not deny justice to your poor people in their lawsuits. ⁷Have nothing to do with a false charge and do not put an innocent or honest person to death, for I will not acquit the guilty.

⁸"Do not accept a bribe, for a bribe blinds those who see and twists the words of the righteous.

⁹"Do not oppress an alien; you yourselves know how it feels to be aliens, because you were aliens in Egypt.

¹⁰"For six years you are to sow your fields and harvest the crops, ¹¹but during the seventh year let the land lie unplowed and unused. Then the poor among your people may get food from it, and the wild animals may eat what they leave. Do the same with your vineyard and your olive grove.

Various Laws Regarding Violent Acts (21:12–17, 22–27)

God's expands the sixth commandment on murder in the first few verses of this passage. The Lord recognizes that some deaths are unintentional and not premeditated. Murder is a very serious act against another human being. Human life is precious and violates the Ten Commandments. Each person is made in the image of God. Some portion of God's likeness is found in all of us. To destroy a life casually—in retaliation, anger, meanness, or without thought for the fact that God forbids murder—is a sin.

> *Genuine faith acts out its belief in daily living.*

Verse 13 can be linked to 21:18–19. Sometimes a person kills someone unintentionally. Such an act, while still very serious, is not viewed by God in the same way as if the murder occurred on purpose or was plotted.

In all likelihood, prior to this law, some might have felt justified in avenging an unintentional death. Suppose two men were struggling or in a dispute. The men might be from different tribes or clans or from different families within the clan or tribe. One man strikes a blow and the other man falls, hitting his head on a rock. Subsequently, the injured man dies from the head injury. The dead man's family may go looking for the one who struck the blow. Finding him, they proceed to kill the man, his wife, any parents living with them, and the children. God wanted to stop such feuds before they could begin.

God set up a justice system that would take into account the circumstances of a death. A premeditated murder was punishable by death. Then, the matter was ended. No other family or clan members were to die. The guilty party received justice for his cruelty. However, if the death was inadvertent, the person who struck the blow would be held liable for lost wages, time of recovery, and any cost of caring for the injured party.

> *"It is not what I do not understand in the Bible that bothers me; it is what I do understand that bothers me."*

Violent acts against a father and mother were punishable by death. Attacking one's parents in a physical or threatening way was reprehensible to God. Verses 15 and 17 go together. In relation to the fifth commandment, we are commanded not only to respect our parents but also to never harm them physically. Even in our society, we find harming one's parents to be unthinkable. While children grow up to be as strong as or stronger than their aging parents, such new strength or physical force must never be used against parents.

Parents deserve respect and honor at every age. Even a parent whose behavior is obnoxious or hurtful can still be treated with dignity, honor, and respect while being rebuked with firmness. It may be that the parent would respond belligerently, but an adult child can turn a deaf ear to such comments.

The principle is a timeless truth. Your parents cared for you when a few hours of neglect would have been detrimental to your existence. They cared for you through sicknesses, disappointments, failures, and difficulties. A Christian returns that unselfish love by tolerance and seeing that parents receive the very best care throughout their lives.

In 21:16, kidnapping is addressed. Kidnapping in this passage involves taking a person by force and selling him into slavery. Because it is not the result of any misdeed of the person who is kidnapped, the admonition is to prevent abuse of power over the weak and less influential. In our society, one is prevented from selling anyone into slavery for any reason. However, the probation against kidnapping is still relevant.

Exodus 21:22–25 involves an interesting passage for modern society. The passage includes the unusual violence that causes the destruction of an unborn child. If a person harms a pregnant woman so severely that she gives birth prematurely (NASB and NRSV translate this as "miscarriage"), but no harm comes to the injured mother, the offender will pay a fine—within reason—to the husband for the loss of the child. However, if the mother dies, the law of retaliation is to be applied. This law limited the punishment to the exact amount of harm done to another person. If the injury resulted in death, then death was the penalty. If one lost a tooth, eye, or hand, then the offender could lose the exact same body parts, but no more. If the injury caused a bruise or wound, then a bruise or wound could be inflicted on the offender in the exact same spot with the exact same damage.

Abortion opponents point to this passage as an example of how God values the unborn child. The unborn developing fetus or embryo certainly has worth to God. The length to which each denominational group, local church, or individual Christian is willing to go in applying this principle regarding the embryonic child varies, though. Still, the passage is clear that the unborn child has worth in the sight of God. The unborn baby is not just tissue like an appendix. It is some form or stage of humanity.

Unborn babies ought not to be aborted as a simple means of birth control. Once a child is conceived, God believes the unborn baby has worth. Like capital punishment and war, abortion ought to be a last resort rather than a first and easy answer. Abortion is a very serious matter and should occur more rarely than it does in our society.

> To destroy a life casually—in retaliation, anger, meanness, or without thought for the fact that God forbids murder—is a sin.

As in Exodus 21:22–25, the law of retaliation is used in verses 26–27 with regard to causing bodily harm to the slave. The text does not indicate that someone other than the owner caused the bodily harm. Consequently, even owners must not harm their own slaves. Slaves were considered property and had few, if any, rights before the covenant code. Through the laws in these verses, God was giving worth to a slave that was not known before. It was an improvement over previous slavery conditions. While we should not use this passage to justify slavery as some of our ancestors did, we can use this teaching in our modern lives to demonstrate that even the poor, helpless, or disadvantaged still have dignity and worth. A common street person in your city should receive the same justice and respect as the city mayor.

In the covenant code, social status or position did not exempt anyone from being under the same law of retaliation as anyone else. Justice must

Cultural and Timeless Truth

Various denominations often seize on a specific teaching found in Scripture and make that normative for their understanding of how to live the Christian life. For instance, the Scripture says, "I also want women to dress modestly, with decency and propriety, not with braided hair or gold or pearls or expensive clothes" (1 Timothy 2:9). When is the last time you heard a sermon admonishing women not to braid their hair or wear expensive clothes, gold, or pearls?

We generally consider the illustrations Paul gave in that verse to be cultural in nature. However, there is a timeless truth in the first part of the Scripture passage. The admonition is against dressing in a vulgar or crude fashion.

Within Scripture are many instances of teachings that are primarily cultural and not intended for literal adherence in every age. The difficulty is in determining what is cultural and what is a timeless truth. Deciding between cultural and timeless truth has always been in dispute. On some such issues, there will never be universal Christian agreement. In such matters, we do well to begin with prayer and study.

---

be equal if it is to be called *justice*. Otherwise, the rich and powerful would not be subject to the same laws as the rest of us.

Remember, the specific meaning of these laws was related to the culture of that day. Nevertheless, we are seeking the timeless truth in each cultural issue.

Various Laws Regarding Social Responsibility (22:21—23:11)

This passage of Scripture covers a hodgepodge of laws over many social issues. All of them revolve around how we treat others in daily living.

The first teaching has to do with foreigners, widows, and orphans (22:21–24; see also 23:9). God declared that his followers were not to mistreat people who were different from them. The New International Version translates the Hebrew word as "alien" (also NRSV). The New American Standard Bible translates it as "stranger." The basic meaning of the word is *sojourner*. There are two kinds of sojourners in

> We must treat foreigners with respect and Christian courtesy.

every nation—foreigners who are permanent residents and those who are temporarily visiting in the land.

Foreigners by nature are subject to unusual social pressures. Customs, language, mores, and societal politeness are difficult for a non-native. God reminded the Israelites that they were once sojourners in Egypt. Therefore, the Hebrews should remember how Pharaoh mistreated them and took advantage of them.

All American citizens who are not pureblood Native Americans were at one time immigrants. Our ancestors came to America hoping for a better life. Their first years likely were difficult and filled with discouragement. Most groups have been hated by those already in America before their group arrived. Each group of immigrants tended to turn the same distrust, bitterness, and disdain toward each newly arriving group.

God wants his people to break this cycle. We must treat foreigners with respect and Christian courtesy.

Widows and orphans are a most important group of people to God. Ancient Hebrew society had no welfare, Medicare, Social Security, or other government assistance. So, widows and orphans were often destitute. They were forgotten—or worse yet, neglected. God did not forget them, however. God admonished his people to remember and care for them. Even today, a person in the church can lose a spouse and feel he or she must drop out of married adult classes where their friends still have spouses. This must not happen. If the person chooses to move to a "singles" class, that is one thing. However, to impose a singles class on another is thoughtless. God doesn't treat people like that, and God doesn't want us to treat them that way either.

God set up a justice system that would take into account the circumstances of a death.

The matter of lending money or goods to a needy person is addressed in 22:25–27. Notice the care that God required of the lender. The lender was not to charge interest to a needy person. God did not forbid a professional moneylender from charging interest, but God did prevent the ordinary neighbor from charging interest. A lender might require a pledge of one's cloak—an outer garment like a coat. Cloaks among the poor were hard to come by. A person might own only two cloaks in an entire lifetime. A cloak was also a bed cover for the poor at night. To take one's cloak was to take away a person's physical welfare. God said the lender must return the cloak at the time the person needs it so that the person does not suffer unnecessarily—in this case, miss sleep because of a cold night.

One can easily see the principle for which God is concerned. God does not want harm to come to a poor person while he or she is trying to earn enough to provide for self or family.

Likewise, God was concerned about gossip and false witnessing (23:1–2). Having addressed this in the ninth commandment, God enlarged the teaching. False testimony is never from God. Gossip is a devilish device. James 3:6 says the tongue is like a forest fire. It is set on fire by hell itself. A true Christian guards against slander, gossip, and the telling of lies. Because such things destroy one's character and reputation, God lists them as evil.

The covenant code speaks of correct behavior toward an enemy. If an Israelite were to see an enemy's ox or donkey wandering off or fallen down because of being hurt, he was to do something about it (Exod. 23:4–5). The Israelite could lead the animal back to his enemy's residence or give aid to the hurt animal. Behaving in a godly manner toward one's enemies may be one of the hardest things God requires of believers. Jesus also requires similar conduct.

> . . . Christ makes it clear that we are to treat our enemies better than they would treat us.

We are to pray for and love our enemies (Matthew 5:43–44). This teaching is very hard to follow. Yet Christ makes it clear that we are to treat our enemies better than they would treat us.

QUESTIONS

1. How much respect and honor should be given to a difficult parent?

2. Have you ever served on a jury where you had to determine a just decision in a personal injury suit?

3. Do you believe that abortion is ever justified in God's eyes?

4. How well do you feel about immigrants coming to America? How do you treat illegal immigrants?

5. Do you think you should charge interest to a needy person?

6. How well do you treat people whom you consider to be antagonistic toward you?

Called to Worship Only God

"Worship wars" may be a poorly chosen and unfortunate phrase, but it does denote that one of the major issues facing believers today is how to worship God. Many churches are re-evaluating what they do and making decisions about possible changes in the way they approach God in worship.

This unit of study is based on the last sixteen chapters in the Book of Exodus (25—40). The key focus is on worship. This material describes both inappropriate worship and worship that follows the instructions of God. The first lesson, from Exodus 32, explores what happens when we fail to worship only God. The Israelites failed in that responsibility and were given a second chance only through the powerful intercession of their great leader Moses.

The second lesson, from Exodus 34, provides the process of Israel's getting that second chance or starting over in their relationship with God. God chose to renew his covenant with the Israelites and reaffirmed guidelines for them, especially in the area of worship.

The final lesson is drawn from the remainder of the material in Exodus 25—40. These chapters concern God's instructions for building a worship structure (the tabernacle) as well as the furniture that would be placed in it. They also include guidelines for the priests (their clothing and practices) and directions on how to worship God in this new structure. God guided the Hebrews in this process so that they could be privileged to have him dwell among them.[1]

Use these lessons to stimulate your thinking about how you might improve your private worship and how you can better prepare to experience God in corporate worship.

UNIT FOUR, CALLED TO WORSHIP ONLY GOD

Lesson 11 A Broken Covenant and
                a Second Chance   Exodus 32:7–34
Lesson 12 Starting Over   Exodus 34:1–28
Lesson 13 God Dwelling Among Us   Exodus 25:1–8;
                                        29:43–46; 33:7–11,
                                        14–16; 40:16–38

NOTES

1. Unless otherwise indicated, all Scripture quotations in this unit of study are from the New International Version.

Focal Text
Exodus 32:7–34

Background
Exodus 32

Main Idea
When the people broke God's covenant, God gave them another chance through Moses' intercession.

Question to Explore
How does forgiveness come?

Study Aim
To recognize the seriousness of sin and the way in which forgiveness comes

Study and Action Emphases

- Affirm the Bible as our authoritative guide for life and ministry
- Share the gospel with all people
- Develop a growing, vibrant faith
- Equip people for servant leadership

LESSON ELEVEN

A Broken Covenant and a Second Chance

Quick Read
The Israelites did not keep their promise to obey God's covenant demands. Moses pleaded with God to give them a second chance.

Recently several university administrations and boards of regents were confronted with tough decisions concerning the careers of talented coaches as a result of accusations of moral misbehavior. One of these accused coaches pleaded his case at a press conference. He admitted to his wrongdoing but, at the same time, declared that he deserved a second chance.

Of course, no one is perfect. Each of us disobeys God's instructions for our lives. We often fail to be the family member or the believer in Jesus that we know we should be. Do we deserve a second chance, though?

At Mount Sinai God invited the Israelites to enter into a covenant agreement with him (Exodus 19). They accepted God's invitation and agreed to live by God's principles (Exod. 20). Moses served as the mediator between Israel and God in this covenant-making process. On one of Moses' trips up the sacred mountain to receive instructions from God, he took Joshua with him and left the Israelites under the care of Aaron and Hur (24:14). While the text of Exodus 24:15—31:18 contains the instructions that Moses received on the mountain, the flow of the story line in Exodus 24:14 continues in 32:1.

Moses remained on the mountain for more than a month (24:18), and God's people became impatient. They prevailed on Aaron to lead them into making a visible god, one they could worship. Aaron responded favorably to their request. They made an idol in the shape of a calf and offered worship to it (32:1–6). Their action threatened the covenant relationship that God had just made with them. It represented an overt and flagrant act of disobedience rather than an accidental straying from God.

Exodus 32:7–34

⁷Then the LORD said to Moses, "Go down, because your people, whom you brought up out of Egypt, have become corrupt. ⁸They have been quick to turn away from what I commanded them and have made themselves an idol cast in the shape of a calf. They have bowed down to it and sacrificed to it and have said, 'These are your gods, O Israel, who brought you up out of Egypt.'

⁹"I have seen these people," the LORD said to Moses, "and they are a stiff-necked people. ¹⁰Now leave me alone so that my anger may burn against them and that I may destroy them. Then I will make you into a great nation."

¹¹But Moses sought the favor of the LORD his God. "O LORD," he said, "why should your anger burn against your people, whom you brought

out of Egypt with great power and a mighty hand? [12]Why should the Egyptians say, 'It was with evil intent that he brought them out, to kill them in the mountains and to wipe them off the face of the earth'? Turn from your fierce anger; relent and do not bring disaster on your people. [13]Remember your servants Abraham, Isaac and Israel, to whom you swore by your own self: 'I will make your descendants as numerous as the stars in the sky and I will give your descendants all this land I promised them, and it will be their inheritance forever.'" [14]Then the LORD relented and did not bring on his people the disaster he had threatened.

[15]Moses turned and went down the mountain with the two tablets of the Testimony in his hands. They were inscribed on both sides, front and back. [16]The tablets were the work of God; the writing was the writing of God, engraved on the tablets.

[17]When Joshua heard the noise of the people shouting, he said to Moses, "There is the sound of war in the camp."

[18]Moses replied:

"It is not the sound of victory,
it is not the sound of defeat;
it is the sound of singing that I hear."

[19]When Moses approached the camp and saw the calf and the dancing, his anger burned and he threw the tablets out of his hands, breaking them to pieces at the foot of the mountain. [20]And he took the calf they had made and burned it in the fire; then he ground it to powder, scattered it on the water and made the Israelites drink it.

[21]He said to Aaron, "What did these people do to you, that you led them into such great sin?"

[22]"Do not be angry, my lord," Aaron answered. "You know how prone these people are to evil. [23]They said to me, 'Make us gods who will go before us. As for this fellow Moses who brought us up out of Egypt, we don't know what has happened to him.' [24]So I told them, 'Whoever has any gold jewelry, take it off.' Then they gave me the gold, and I threw it into the fire, and out came this calf!"

[25]Moses saw that the people were running wild and that Aaron had let them get out of control and so become a laughingstock to their enemies. [26]So he stood at the entrance to the camp and said, "Whoever is for the LORD, come to me." And all the Levites rallied to him.

[27]Then he said to them, "This is what the LORD, the God of Israel, says: 'Each man strap a sword to his side. Go back and forth through the camp from one end to the other, each killing his brother and friend and neighbor.'" [28]The Levites did as Moses commanded, and that day about three thousand of the people died. [29]Then Moses said, "You have been set

apart to the LORD today, for you were against your own sons and brothers, and he has blessed you this day."

[30]The next day Moses said to the people, "You have committed a great sin. But now I will go up to the LORD; perhaps I can make atonement for your sin."

[31]So Moses went back to the LORD and said, "Oh, what a great sin these people have committed! They have made themselves gods of gold. [32]But now, please forgive their sin—but if not, then blot me out of the book you have written."

[33]The LORD replied to Moses, "Whoever has sinned against me I will blot out of my book. [34]Now go, lead the people to the place I spoke of, and my angel will go before you. However, when the time comes for me to punish, I will punish them for their sin."

A Broken Covenant: The Response of God (32:7–10)

The strong response of God demonstrates the seriousness of the people's actions. His response included two elements: the announcement or indictment of their sinful actions and the resulting punishment to be carried out.

The Israelites broke their covenant promise to God at their first opportunity.

God instructed Moses to descend the mountain because something terrible had occurred. The selection of pronouns says it all. God refused to claim them. To Moses he made this indictment against "*your* people, whom *you* brought up out of Egypt" (32:7, italics for emphasis). Contrast this statement with other texts where God asserted that he himself delivered Israel out of Egypt and that Israel was his precious possession (19:3–6; 20:2).

The Israelites were no longer acting like the people of God, for they had become "corrupt" (32:7). The most basic meaning of this word is *to destroy physically or bring to ruin*. It also signifies, as here, a morally or spiritually destructive act. The Israelites had done something that altered their covenant relationship to God. Previously, they had pledged their obedience to God. They had now violated that pledge.

This violation of their pledge did not occur after a long and faithful relationship with God; rather, they were "quick to turn away" (32:8). We would be appalled if a newlywed broke his or her marriage vow by being unfaithful on the honeymoon. We would be shocked if an employee began distributing résumés to other companies during the initial orientation process at a new job. The Israelites broke their covenant promise to God at their first opportunity. This narrative echoes the event of Genesis 3. The newly-created man and woman rebelled against their Maker at the first opportunity to do so and thus brought to ruin their perfect relationship with God.

Sin breaks fellowship with God and creates a barrier between the Creator and those created.

The specific violation of the Israelites' pledge concerned the making of "an idol cast in the shape of a calf" (32:8). They may have wanted this calf to serve as a physical representation of their invisible God (a violation of the second commandment, 20:4), or the idol may have served as a substitute for their God (a violation of the first commandment, 20:3). God condemned their activity because they directed acts of worship toward the calf and attributed to this calf their deliverance from Egypt.

After declaring his accusations against the Israelites, God announced what their punishment would be. God was so angry and disappointed with the idolatry of the people that he determined to "destroy" them (32:10). This verb is the common word for eating food. It is a graphic way to describe annihilation. Even as one bites, chews, and swallows (or consumes) food, God announced that he would completely consume or devour these people. He would then use Moses as the "father" of a new people who would obey God.

Atonement

The Bible says that human sinfulness has created a barrier between God and us, an obstacle to any fulfilling relationship. Some ancient cultures believed that the obstacles between divine and human beings came from the side of the divine. The gods were angry and needed to be pacified or satisfied. The Israelites correctly understood that the ill effects of sin itself created this barrier. It was not within God.

Atonement is the word denoting the removal of that sin-caused barrier. In the Old Testament period God established the sacrificial system as the vehicle to bring about atonement. Israelites offered these gifts to God in order for the personal relationship between God and God's creation to be restored.

In the New Testament, atonement is achieved not through offering gifts to God but rather results from God's offering the gift of his Son to us. We have the opportunity of being reconciled (at one) with God through the perfect obedience of Jesus in his life, death, and resurrection.

God instructed Moses to leave him alone, that is, not to interfere with him as he carried out this drastic punishment. This statement may implic-

God is steadfast and constant in his love and will change his mind or relent in order to remain true to his unchangeable purpose.

itly contain God's invitation to Moses to intervene. It at least raises the possibility that Moses can participate in the divine deliberation.

Our sins have a serious negative effect on our relationship with God. Sin breaks fellowship with God and creates a barrier between the Creator and those created. In order for some kind of reconciliation or restoration to occur, that barrier must be removed. God's mechanism for dealing with that barrier is forgiveness. So, how is forgiveness possible?

The Plea of Moses for a Second Chance (32:11–14)

Here we see Moses at his best as he pleaded with God not to destroy the Israelites. The structure of these verses reveals the daring boldness of Moses.

Moses offered God three reasons he should not carry out his announced punishment.

- First, the destruction of the Israelites would in some way waste or undo the mighty act of God in delivering the Israelites from Egyptian slavery and in creating this people for himself (32:11 compared with 32:7).
- Second, Moses argued that this punishment would damage the reputation of God among the Egyptians. They would most certainly misunderstand the cause and effect dynamics of Israel's destruction (32:12).
- Finally, Moses believed that it would result in God's inability to fulfill the promise of countless descendants that he had made to the ancestors (32:13; Genesis 15:5).

Moses did have an impact on God's decision. In fact "the LORD relented," determining not to carry out the total destruction of the Israelites as he had planned (Exod. 32:14). (The King James Version renders this verse, "And the Lord repented of the evil which he thought to do unto his people.")

The biblical witness in both the Old and New Testaments is that God never repents of sin. He never has the need to do so. All of God's actions are fully justified and appropriate. Repentance from sin involves a twofold process. It begins with an internal emotional attitude of regret over the presence of sinful behavior. That inner regret then results in a change of behavior or a turning away from sin.

"Relent" or "relented" (32:12, 14) translates a Hebrew word that means *to suffer grief or sadness, to be moved with pity or compassion, and to comfort or console.* It also denotes *to be sorry for some event or situation.* In the vast majority of the cases in which this word occurs in the Old Testament, God is the subject. The sense is that God feels compassion toward his human creation when they rebel against him. That compassion causes God to change his mind or intent to carry out extensive judgment in response to a plea or intercession. When God relents (reverses a previous decision or declaration), God always does so in a way that is in accord with his righteous and just character. God is steadfast and constant in his love and will change his mind or relent in order to remain true to his unchangeable purpose.

Is that a creative excuse or what?

Moses interceded with God in Israel's behalf. He pleaded their case. Forgiveness becomes a possibility when someone intercedes with God. Ultimately this mediator function or role would be filled by God himself through God's Son (1 Timothy 2:5).

A Broken Covenant: The Response of Moses (32:15–29)

After pleading with God in behalf of Israel, Moses descended the mountain. He carried the "two tablets of the Testimony" (32:15), on which were written the Ten Commandments. The phrases of verse 16 denote the authority of these commandments. They had their origin in God. He was the source for Israel's instructions.

Seeing something tends to be more emotionally stirring than merely hearing about it. God had related the situation to Moses, but now Moses saw it for himself. When Moses saw the idolatrous (and probably immoral) worship, he experienced the same reaction as God had (compare 32:19 with 32:10).

Moses' anger produced two actions (32:19–20). The physical breaking of the stone tablets is symbolic of the breaking of the covenant relationship

The Process of Forgiveness

One of the most sacred human relationships is that of marriage. Suppose that a husband violates his wife's trust by having a romantic relationship with another woman. He realizes that he has strayed from God's design for his life. He ends the affair and requests forgiveness from his wife.

Does the husband deserve a second chance? What must occur in order for forgiveness to be granted and received? What can or should the wife require of her mate? Is there one and only one particular strategy that must be followed in order for forgiveness to happen?

that God had established with God's people. Moses then took steps to destroy completely the idol that the people had made. The fact that Moses "burned it in the fire" and "ground it to powder" (32:20) may intimate that the calf idol consisted of a wooden framework overlaid with gold.

Moses then proceeded to deal with his brother Aaron, the one who had been responsible for the people during his absence. Aaron recounted the events to Moses. The interesting thing to note is that he was accurate in telling Moses what had happened until he came to the matter of his own involvement. He completely denied any responsibility for the creation of this idol. He asserted that all he did was to receive the gold and put it in the fire, "and out came this calf" (32:24).

Moses wanted either to be destroyed with them or to be punished by God in their place.

Is that a creative excuse or what? Again this narrative reminds us of Genesis 3 where the man and woman put the blame for their error on anybody else except themselves.

Moses had pleaded with God not to destroy the people completely, but he did realize that they deserved some punishment (32:25–29). He challenged all who wanted to be totally loyal to God to express it publicly. The text states that many of the Levites (the tribe of Moses and Aaron) did express their loyalty to God. Moses utilized them to punish others who refused to show any repentance. Moses implemented this punishment with the authority of God (32:27).

The fact that three thousand died on that day of punishment reveals the seriousness of sin against God and the dreadful cost of it. Even though God desires to forgive our sin, God's justice requires that sin be punished.

The Plan of God for a Second Chance (32:30–34)

In these verses Moses exhibited the characteristics of a true leader. The people probably blamed Aaron for this mess, while Aaron blamed the fire itself. Moses placed the blame where it belonged, on the shoulders of each individual who participated in the idolatry. Moses entertained the idea of returning to meet God on the mountain in order to "make atonement for your sin" (32:30). I do not think Moses was referring to any sacrificial act; rather he hoped he could convince God not to carry out the punishment God had announced previously.

Moses again committed himself to represent the people before God. Moses had now seen what God had seen, and he agreed with God that it was a grievous and sad transgression (32:30). Moses did not waste words. He begged God to forgive them. "Forgive" (32:32) literally means *to lift up*. Moses asked God to remove the burden and guilt of their sins. The dash in the translation "please forgive their sin—but if not" signifies that it is an incomplete thought. Moses struggled with this request and could hardly compose himself in order to express his passionate desires.

> *Sin creates a barrier that only the forgiveness of God can remove.*

Moses then declared that if God refused to forgive the Israelites, he wanted God "to blot me out of the book you have written" (32:32). Moses wanted either to be destroyed with them or to be punished by God in their place. Some ancient cities had the custom of keeping a book in which were written all of the names (and good deeds) of the citizens. If the book did not contain someone's name, then that person did not enjoy the privileges afforded the citizens of the city. The prophets used the practice to picture the joy of being included among the people of God (Isa. 4:3; Jer. 22:30).

God did not accept Moses' offer to be punished in the place of the Israelites. He asserted the principle of individual accountability for sins. At the same time God chose not to destroy them. The reader must conclude that God decided to express his love by forgiving his people. He determined to continue to lead them to the land that he had promised them. He would continue to grant them the privilege of enjoying his accompanying presence (32:34).

Sin is a serious affront to God and has serious consequences. Sin creates a barrier that only the forgiveness of God can remove. The forgiveness

God offers us is made possible by the life, death, and resurrection of Jesus, who gave his life for us and pleads with God in our behalf.

QUESTIONS

1. What is your reaction to the assertion that the coach made when attempting to keep his job? Does everybody deserve a second chance? If so, what is the nature of a second chance?

2. How would you compare and contrast Moses and Jesus in their respective roles as mediator/intercessor?

3. What role does intercessory prayer play in the process of one experiencing the saving forgiveness of Jesus Christ?

4. We speak in terms of the grace of God being a free gift. Is grace really free?

Focal Text

Exodus 34:1–28

Background

Exodus 34

Main Idea

Making a fresh start spiritually calls for renewing our commitment to God's covenant.

Question to Explore

When have you found it necessary to renew your commitment to God's covenant?

Study Aim

To recall experiences of covenant renewal in my life

Study and Action Emphases

- Affirm the Bible as our authoritative guide for life and ministry
- Develop a growing, vibrant faith
- Equip people for servant leadership

LESSON TWELVE

Starting Over

Quick Read

God forgave the Israelites for their idolatrous worship. That reality gave them the privilege of "starting over" in their covenant relationship with God.

I ran and completed my first marathon (26.2 miles) in 1985 in The Woodlands (north of Houston, Texas). I have run a total of only two in my life, but I love the sound of that phrase "completed my first marathon." Unlike the course for most marathons, this one consisted of a double loop. When you completed 13.1 miles, you were back at the beginning point and had the privilege of "starting over" or running that same course again.

As I started over that day, I knew that the course with all of its twists and turns was the same, but I also realized that some things had changed. My energy level had diminished somewhat. My muscles were beginning to ache. I was not as fresh and excited as before. In addition, the environment around me had changed. I did not see the same runners with whom I had begun the run. Some were way ahead of me. Others were behind me. Some had dropped out along the way. Starting over to complete that marathon had some elements of sameness and also difference.

The Israelites had sinned against God (Exodus 32:1–6). God forgave them and then took the initiative to make a new start with them. Exodus 34 reveals that starting over has some elements of sameness but also a dimension of difference. God's grace and God's promises as the foundations of the covenant are constant. Even though forgiveness can be received, the slate cannot be wiped completely clean of all of the circumstances of rebellion. As a result, the landscape has changed. In Exodus 34, some of God's directions to Moses are slightly different from those found in Exodus 19—20. Some of the Israelites were no longer present, having been punished (Exod. 32:25–29). The principles themselves also differ from the principles of chapter 20.

Exodus 34:1–28

[1]The LORD said to Moses, "Chisel out two stone tablets like the first ones, and I will write on them the words that were on the first tablets, which you broke. [2]Be ready in the morning, and then come up on Mount Sinai. Present yourself to me there on top of the mountain. [3]No one is to come with you or be seen anywhere on the mountain; not even the flocks and herds may graze in front of the mountain."

[4]So Moses chiseled out two stone tablets like the first ones and went up Mount Sinai early in the morning, as the LORD had commanded him; and he carried the two stone tablets in his hands. [5]Then the LORD came down in the cloud and stood there with him and proclaimed his name, the LORD. [6]And he passed in front of Moses, proclaiming, "The LORD, the

LORD, the compassionate and gracious God, slow to anger, abounding in love and faithfulness, [7]maintaining love to thousands, and forgiving wickedness, rebellion and sin. Yet he does not leave the guilty unpunished; he punishes the children and their children for the sin of the fathers to the third and fourth generation."

[8]Moses bowed to the ground at once and worshiped. [9]"O Lord, if I have found favor in your eyes," he said, "then let the Lord go with us. Although this is a stiff-necked people, forgive our wickedness and our sin, and take us as your inheritance."

[10]Then the LORD said: "I am making a covenant with you. Before all your people I will do wonders never before done in any nation in all the world. The people you live among will see how awesome is the work that I, the LORD, will do for you. [11]Obey what I command you today. I will drive out before you the Amorites, Canaanites, Hittites, Perizzites, Hivites and Jebusites. [12]Be careful not to make a treaty with those who live in the land where you are going, or they will be a snare among you. [13]Break down their altars, smash their sacred stones and cut down their Asherah poles. [14]Do not worship any other god, for the LORD, whose name is Jealous, is a jealous God.

[15]"Be careful not to make a treaty with those who live in the land; for when they prostitute themselves to their gods and sacrifice to them, they will invite you and you will eat their sacrifices. [16]And when you choose some of their daughters as wives for your sons and those daughters prostitute themselves to their gods, they will lead your sons to do the same.

[17]"Do not make cast idols.

[18]"Celebrate the Feast of Unleavened Bread. For seven days eat bread made without yeast, as I commanded you. Do this at the appointed time in the month of Abib, for in that month you came out of Egypt.

[19]"The first offspring of every womb belongs to me, including all the firstborn males of your livestock, whether from herd or flock. [20]Redeem the firstborn donkey with a lamb, but if you do not redeem it, break its neck. Redeem all your firstborn sons.

"No one is to appear before me empty-handed.

[21]"Six days you shall labor, but on the seventh day you shall rest; even during the plowing season and harvest you must rest.

[22]"Celebrate the Feast of Weeks with the firstfruits of the wheat harvest, and the Feast of Ingathering at the turn of the year. [23]Three times a year all your men are to appear before the Sovereign LORD, the God of Israel. [24]I will drive out nations before you and enlarge your territory, and no one will covet your land when you go up three times each year to appear before the LORD your God.

---

²⁵"Do not offer the blood of a sacrifice to me along with anything containing yeast, and do not let any of the sacrifice from the Passover Feast remain until morning.

²⁶"Bring the best of the firstfruits of your soil to the house of the LORD your God.

"Do not cook a young goat in its mother's milk."

²⁷Then the LORD said to Moses, "Write down these words, for in accordance with these words I have made a covenant with you and with Israel." ²⁸Moses was there with the LORD forty days and forty nights without eating bread or drinking water. And he wrote on the tablets the words of the covenant—the Ten Commandments.

God's Character Revealed Again (34:1–7)

Starting over is never quite identical to the initial start or beginning. Israel had broken the provisions of God's covenant, and Moses had physically broken the stone tablets that contained those principles (32:15–20). God was ready to write those principles again (34:1). This time, however, Moses was responsible for providing the stone tablets (34:1; see 24:12). In addition to that, he was to ascend Sinai by himself this time (34:3; see 24:1). Moses obeyed God without questioning him about the changes in format (34:4).

God graciously revealed himself again to Moses. It was different from the way that God revealed himself when God first gave Israel the Ten Commandments. On that occasion God had manifested his awesome power as Mount Sinai became the scene of clouds, fire, the thunder and lightning of a storm, and the violent shaking of an earthquake (19:16–19). On this occasion he demonstrated his awesome holiness as expressed in his grace and forgiveness (34:5–7). That dimension of God's character was the one that Israel most needed to hear.

Even though forgiveness can be received, the slate cannot be wiped completely clean of all of the circumstances of rebellion.

Several years ago when my oldest son was then a preschooler, I had to return home in the middle of the day to retrieve something. It was a "providential" moment for Tim, who stayed next door with our neighbor and church member. He also wanted to retrieve something that he had forgotten that day, his "mean green machine." We both accomplished our respective missions. As Tim pedaled his prize transportation back toward

Mrs. Lucille's house, he looked over his shoulder and yelled, "Thanks, Dad, you are always around when I need you."

God is not only always around when we need him, but he is present in exactly the way that we need him. Here he was "around" for Israel in the way that they needed him.

Starting over is never quite identical to the initial start or beginning.

The Lord "came down in the cloud" (34:5). The Bible frequently uses clouds to symbolize God's presence but also to imply his mystery. The combination of the verbs "came down" and "proclaimed" (34:5) along with "passed in front of" and "proclaiming" (34:6) suggests that it was more a verbal than a visual revelation. It was a powerful, defining revelation concerning the name or nature of God not shared with anyone before or after Moses.

Verses 6–7 assert God's wonderful nature in statements that reveal God's generosity.

- "Compassionate" translates a verb associated with the noun for *womb*. It describes the mother's strong and protective love for that which comes forth from her own body.
- "Gracious" reminds us that God is not forced to love or act kindly toward us. God lavishes his kindness upon us because God chooses to do so.
- "Slow to anger" is literally *long nosed*. The Hebrews observed that someone who was impatient or angry took short, choppy breaths, while someone who was relaxed did slow, deep breathing. While being *short nosed* meant to be impatient with others, *long nosed* denoted a patient and understanding person.
- "Love" renders a very prominent word in the Old Testament (*hesed*). This word does not describe love in its emotional or affectionate dimension. The Hebrew people used this word only with regard to a previously made promise or established covenant bond. It thus referred to the loyalty or willingness to live up to the commitment that one had made. This loyalty trait was often paired with *truth*, referring to the complete trustworthiness and reliability of God that guaranteed his loyalty. The word "love" in verse 6 emphasizes the quality of God's committed loyalty, while the phrase "maintaining love to thousands" (34:7) points to the quantity of that loyalty. God's covenant faithfulness was extended indefinitely.

- "Forgiving wickedness," the final statement of these seven words about God's generosity, concerns the forgiving nature of God. "Wickedness, rebellion, and sin" are the three most common terms in the Old Testament for unfaithfulness. The sense is that the forgiveness of God is sufficient to cover all manner of sinfulness.

Although God is willing to forgive our sins, the latter part of verse 7 emphasizes that God is not pleased with them. In fact, God has determined to "not leave the guilty unpunished" (34:7). The grammatical form here is the strongest expression of certainty that the Hebrew language possesses. Thus, we must understand God's generosity or grace in balance with his severity or judgment of sin. The expression concerning the intergenerational nature of sin and punishment does not mean that God directly punishes one person for the sins of another person; rather, it declares that sin has its consequences in its negative influence on others. Ezekiel 18:1–4 clearly announces the truth that God punishes each of us for our own sins and not for the sins of others.

> . . . The forgiveness of God is sufficient to cover all manner of sinfulness.

These important sentiments are quoted directly or indirectly in such passages as Numbers 14:18; Nehemiah 9:17; Psalm 103:8; 145:8; Jeremiah 32:18–19; and Nahum 1:3. They are also echoed in Deuteronomy 5:9–10;

Demographics of Canaan

Pre-Israelite Canaan was ethnically diverse. Two groups dominated. The Amorites were a Semitic people who occupied the hill country on both sides of the Jordan River and frequently made alliances with other "hill dwellers" such as Hittites and Jebusites. Canaanites (perhaps originally from the Phoenician coast) lent their name to the land between Syria and Egypt. They primarily lived in fortified cities along the Mediterranean coast and in the Plain of Esdraelon between the Mediterranean Sea and the Sea of Galilee.

Ethnic minorities included the Hittites, an Indo-European people who had migrated southward from central Asia and Turkey (some of them at least as early as Abraham). A number of them settled in the southern hill country of Judah around Hebron. The Perizzites (name means *rustic*) probably lived in open or rural spaces between the urban centers. The Hivites are not known outside the Bible. They may have links to the Horites or Hurrians. The Jebusites controlled Jerusalem until the time of David (2 Samuel 5:6).

1 Kings 3:6; Lamentations 3:22; and Daniel 9:4. Whenever God directs us to renew our commitment to him and pledge ourselves to him in a new way, God always teaches us something new about his character and will.

God's Covenant with Israel Affirmed Again (34:8–11)

Moses made a twofold response to this new revelation of God. First, realizing the significance of this divine disclosure, he offered God a genuine attitude of humility and worship. He then interceded with God in behalf of Israel. Moses pleaded with God to express his gracious side to Israel rather than his judging side and thus to forgive their sins. Israel as God's "inheritance" (34:9) signified the role of Israel as God's beloved and personal possession within the promise of granting them a land.

God agreed to renew the covenant with Israel. As a part of God's willingness to start all over with Israel as his covenant partner, God promised to "do wonders never before done" (34:10). The verb designates the action of creation, that work that God alone can do. The language reminds the reader of the awesome and mighty deeds that God had performed in Egypt. On the other hand, it implies that God will do things that as yet

Although God is willing to forgive our sins, God is not pleased with them.

Israel had not seen or experienced. Probably this new work of God would be his leading them into the Promised Land and dispossessing the land's inhabitants (34:11). The collection of these ethnic designations was the typical way to denote the pre-Israelite demographics of Canaan (also see 3:8, 17; 23:23–33).

God's Requirements for Israel Expressed Again (34:12–28)

The general command to obey God (34:11) is made more specific by the instructions found in these verses. The central focus is worship. God reminded them of the wrong ways (34:12–17) and the correct ways (34:18–26) in which God should be worshiped.

The wrong or forbidden ways are divided into guidelines against worshiping other gods and guidelines against inadequate ways of offering worship to the true God. Proactive measures against the temptation to worship other gods involve the command not to enter into any economic or family alliances with the other peoples in Canaan (34:12–13). This warning was sounded frequently in the biblical narrative. The Israelites failed to heed this warning and at great cost (see Judges 2:1–3).

God allowed no interplay with these other peoples because God knew that it could make possible the compromising of their faith. He prohibited worship of any other god because he is a "jealous" God (Exod. 34:14). In the Old Testament, only God is described by this word. The popular concept of jealousy includes a suspicion and apprehension of competition or rivalry from others. It is petty and selfish. We are jealous because we selfishly want something or someone for ourselves. This word is not about such an attitude; rather, it involves passion for others and is demanding of exclusive loyalty for the good of others. God demands religious and worship purity from us because God knows that it will result in our own good. Verse 17 expressly forbids what Israel did in constructing the golden calf.

> *When we realize we are involved in activities that displease God, we must be willing to admit our guilt and allow God to help us start over. . . .*

We sometimes let our lives become interlaced with those of people who do not share our values and spiritual principles. We become intimately involved with them and negatively influenced by them. When we realize we are involved in activities that displease God, we must be willing to admit our guilt and allow God to help us start over and resume our special relationship with Jesus.

God did forbid certain worship practices, but God also provided meaningful ways by which God's people could approach him. Appropriate worship of God rejoices in what God has done. It should focus on God as the giver of grace, recognizing that God is the source of all gifts of personal and material blessing.

On three occasions the Israelites were to celebrate as an entire people the historical and current blessing of God (34:23). In the spring of the year they acknowledged in the observance of Passover and Unleavened Bread the deliverance by God from Egyptian captivity (34:18, 25; see 12:1–23). This feast also celebrated the beginning of the barley harvest. In the summer they rejoiced in the beginning of the wheat harvest (Feast of Weeks, 34:22). At the end of the agricultural year in late summer they remembered God's provision in the wilderness wandering and acknowledged the ingathering of the fruit of the vine (Feast of Ingathering, 34:22).

Renewing Our Commitment

Even as Israel needed to reaffirm her covenant, believers sometimes have the need to make a fresh start spiritually. Renewing our commitment to be faithful to Christ may involve renewal in the following areas:

- A consistency in reading the Bible, individually and with others
- A commitment to be involved in meaningful worship
- A greater sensitivity to personal integrity
- A desire to strengthen a marriage relationship

In addition to these annual celebrations of worship, the Israelites were to remember God's blessings each week by resting on one day (34:21). Whenever they were blessed with the birth of a child or an addition to their herd or flock, they were to offer a sacrifice to God, recognizing that God is the giver of all new life (34:19; see 13:1–16). The significance of not cooking a young goat in its mother's milk is not completely understood (34:26).

Any time can be an appropriate time to ask God to help you gain a fresh perspective of God's grace and give you a chance to start over.

The final two verses in this paragraph provide a summary of this new and reaffirmed covenant that God made with Israel. The chief interpretation issue is the question of the connection between the principles that are announced here and those of Exodus 20:1–17, the summarized principles of the Mosaic covenant. The uncertainty concerns what was written down on this second set of tablets. Was it the principles that we find in Exodus 34:12–26? Was it the Ten Commandments that we find recorded in chapter 20?

Some Old Testament interpreters believe that we find two sets of ten principles in the Book of Exodus. They understand the requirements in this chapter to be arranged into a structure of ten commands. They point out that one set (the Ten Commandments in Exod. 20) is more ethically and spiritually oriented, while the other set (Exod. 34) is more concerned with ritual or worship patterns. In reality it is impossible to understand fully the relationship between these two chapters. It may be that the most that we can conclude is that since the initial covenant breaking concerned sinful worship, the renewal of the covenant focused on worship practices.

Moses continued to be the mediator between God and Israel. He communicated to the people the guidelines in the renewed covenant (34:29–34).

Implications for Today

When is it necessary for believers to start over in their commitment to Jesus, that is, to reaffirm their love and loyalty to him? The need to "start over" may occur when we get busy or distracted by other things and ignore our spiritual component of life. We may need to seek renewal when we become disappointed in others, disillusioned by circumstances, or involved in destructive, sinful behavior. Any time can be an appropriate time to ask God to help you gain a fresh perspective of God's grace and give you a chance to start over.

QUESTIONS

1. Do you agree with the statement, "Even though forgiveness can be received, the slate cannot be wiped completely clean of all of the circumstances of rebellion"? Why or why not?

2. What are some factors that cause people not to seek that "starting over" experience with God when it is needed?

3. Have you ever had an experience in which God revealed himself to you in a timely fashion and in exactly the way that you needed him?

4. What is your favorite seasonal or once-a-year worship celebration? What makes it so meaningful to you?

Focal Text

Exodus 25:1–8; 29:43–46;
33:7–11, 14–16; 40:16–38

Background

Exodus 25:1—31:11;
33; 35:4—40:38

Main Idea

Throughout history,
God has taken measures
to dwell among people
in special ways.

Question to Explore

Where is God?

Study Aim

To state implications of the significance
of the tabernacle and describe ways in
which I sense God's presence today

Study and Action Emphases

- Affirm the Bible as our authoritative guide
  for life and ministry
- Share the gospel with all people
- Develop a growing, vibrant faith

LESSON THIRTEEN

God Dwelling Among Us

Quick Read

God graciously offers himself to us. He also
shares appropriate ways to approach him in
worship. When we follow God's instructions, we
can experience God's intimate presence.

Several years ago I spent a fascinating day taking the tour through the Pentagon in Arlington, Virginia. George Bergstrom was the architect of this Neo-classical style building completed during World War II. This famous building is five floors in height, has five exterior sides, and has an interior divided into five rings. It contains 6.5 million square feet of floor space covering 34 acres. It is the largest office building in the world. The office space, 3.7 million square feet of it, is connected by 17.5 miles of hallways.

The arrangement of two of those offices makes an important symbolic statement. The Chairman of the Joint Chiefs of Staff is the highest-ranking military person who works in the Pentagon. This person has authority over every branch of our military. His office is directly beneath the office occupied by the Secretary of Defense, the highest-ranking civilian who works in the Pentagon. That arrangement makes the declaration that in this country the military is under the control of civilian government.

In constructing a building, form should follow function. The way that a building is designed and built depends on the purpose for which it exists in the first place. God commanded the Israelites to build a worship place in which he would dwell. Because it would serve that important purpose, it had to be built in the way that God directed and in a way that would reveal something of God's nature.

The background of this study includes the rest of the chapters in this book not yet examined in this series of lessons. They comprise almost half of the content of the Book of Exodus. God gave instructions concerning the worship place and the personnel who would serve in it (Exodus 25—31). Moses and the Israelites fully complied with God's instructions (Exod. 35—40).

Exodus 25:1–8

[1]The LORD said to Moses, [2]"Tell the Israelites to bring me an offering. You are to receive the offering for me from each man whose heart prompts him to give. [3]These are the offerings you are to receive from them: gold, silver and bronze; [4]blue, purple and scarlet yarn and fine linen; goat hair; [5]ram skins dyed red and hides of sea cows; acacia wood; [6]olive oil for the light; spices for the anointing oil and for the fragrant incense; [7]and onyx stones and other gems to be mounted on the ephod and breastpiece.

[8]"Then have them make a sanctuary for me, and I will dwell among them.

Exodus 29:43–46

[43]There also I will meet with the Israelites, and the place will be consecrated by my glory.

[44]"So I will consecrate the Tent of Meeting and the altar and will consecrate Aaron and his sons to serve me as priests. [45]Then I will dwell among the Israelites and be their God. [46]They will know that I am the LORD their God, who brought them out of Egypt so that I might dwell among them. I am the LORD their God.

Exodus 33:7–11, 14–16

[7]Now Moses used to take a tent and pitch it outside the camp some distance away, calling it the "tent of meeting." Anyone inquiring of the LORD would go to the tent of meeting outside the camp. [8]And whenever Moses went out to the tent, all the people rose and stood at the entrances to their tents, watching Moses until he entered the tent. [9]As Moses went into the tent, the pillar of cloud would come down and stay at the entrance, while the LORD spoke with Moses. [10]Whenever the people saw the pillar of cloud standing at the entrance to the tent, they all stood and worshiped, each at the entrance to his tent. [11]The LORD would speak to Moses face to face, as a man speaks with his friend. Then Moses would return to the camp, but his young aide Joshua son of Nun did not leave the tent.

. . . .

[14]The LORD replied, "My Presence will go with you, and I will give you rest."

[15]Then Moses said to him, "If your Presence does not go with us, do not send us up from here. [16]How will anyone know that you are pleased with me and with your people unless you go with us? What else will distinguish me and your people from all the other people on the face of the earth?"

Exodus 40:16–38

[16]Moses did everything just as the LORD commanded him.

[17]So the tabernacle was set up on the first day of the first month in the second year. [18]When Moses set up the tabernacle, he put the bases in place, erected the frames, inserted the crossbars and set up the posts. [19]Then he spread the tent over the tabernacle and put the covering over the tent, as the LORD commanded him.

²⁰He took the Testimony and placed it in the ark, attached the poles to the ark and put the atonement cover over it. ²¹Then he brought the ark into the tabernacle and hung the shielding curtain and shielded the ark of the Testimony, as the LORD commanded him.

²²Moses placed the table in the Tent of Meeting on the north side of the tabernacle outside the curtain ²³and set out the bread on it before the LORD, as the LORD commanded him.

²⁴He placed the lampstand in the Tent of Meeting opposite the table on the south side of the tabernacle ²⁵and set up the lamps before the LORD, as the LORD commanded him.

²⁶Moses placed the gold altar in the Tent of Meeting in front of the curtain ²⁷and burned fragrant incense on it, as the LORD commanded him. ²⁸Then he put up the curtain at the entrance to the tabernacle.

²⁹He set the altar of burnt offering near the entrance to the tabernacle, the Tent of Meeting, and offered on it burnt offerings and grain offerings, as the LORD commanded him.

³⁰He placed the basin between the Tent of Meeting and the altar and put water in it for washing, ³¹and Moses and Aaron and his sons used it to wash their hands and feet. ³²They washed whenever they entered the Tent of Meeting or approached the altar, as the LORD commanded Moses.

³³Then Moses set up the courtyard around the tabernacle and altar and put up the curtain at the entrance to the courtyard. And so Moses finished the work.

³⁴Then the cloud covered the Tent of Meeting, and the glory of the LORD filled the tabernacle. ³⁵Moses could not enter the Tent of Meeting because the cloud had settled upon it, and the glory of the LORD filled the tabernacle.

³⁶In all the travels of the Israelites, whenever the cloud lifted from above the tabernacle, they would set out; ³⁷but if the cloud did not lift, they did not set out—until the day it lifted. ³⁸So the cloud of the LORD was over the tabernacle by day, and fire was in the cloud by night, in the sight of all the house of Israel during all their travels.

The Grace of God (25:1–8)

God chose to dwell among God's people. Since God takes the initiative to share himself with us, the logical conclusion is that worship is a gift we are privileged to enjoy. Although we can worship in any place, it is good to have a place that we use uniquely for that purpose.

God's first directive concerned the funding of this new worship place. God invited all of the Israelites to share in this stewardship opportunity. No one was forced to do so. "From each man whose heart prompts him to give" (25:2) reflects the best expression of a serious Baptist emphasis, religious liberty. Worship ceases to be worship when it is made mandatory. Likewise, every element of worship should be expressed voluntarily.

The word underlying "offering" (25:2) comes from a verb meaning to be raised up or lofty. It referred to setting aside a portion of one's entire material wealth for a high and sacred purpose. All Christians should understand the responsibility of using some of their hard-earned income to make possible a place to worship God.

The list of materials that would be needed for the worship place included precious metals, fine linen materials, leathers, wood, oil, spices, and semi-precious stones (25:3–7). Recently liberated slaves could have possessed these kinds of materials only through the grace of God. In fact, God had commanded the securing of these things from the Egyptians (3:21–22; 11:2; 12:35–36). The only reason

> *God's first directive concerned the funding of this new worship place.*

that we have gifts to share with God is that God gives them to us. How sad it is for people to receive material blessings from God and refuse to return to God a portion (offering) of their wealth.

God finally declared the purpose for requesting this offering. "Sanctuary" (25:8) is literally a holy place or a place uniquely set apart for the purpose of expressing the worship of God, who is himself holy. This word was used not only for this worship place but also for every place where God chose to reveal himself (see 15:17; Joshua 24:26; Amos 7:9).

The prepositional phrase "for me" (Exod. 25:8) suggests an incredible but often missed truth. God declared that he would be the beneficiary of the worship and ministry that would be offered there. It is amazing to think that our worship, when appropriately offered, in some way benefits God.

"I will dwell" means *to travel, to dwell,* or *to inhabit a place.* It was a technical term used to describe God's presence among God's people. This word suggested the complete presence of God; however, it did not denote any stable guarantee of God's permanent presence. The God who promised to dwell in this worship place had the freedom to leave. He chose to dwell with Israel because of his grace. This verb provides the noun by which this portable worship place was most commonly known, the "tabernacle" (25:9) or *dwelling place* of God.

Exodus 25:10—31:18 details God's instructions to Israel about how to build the tabernacle and how to clothe the priests who would serve in it. The tabernacle consisted of a courtyard and a structure within the courtyard. The structure was a wooden framework that supported curtains of animal skins and material. It was divided into two rooms. Pieces of furniture were placed within the structure and the courtyard. Since God would dwell in the tabernacle, Israel could experience God's presence when they left Sinai.

The Holiness of God (29:43–46)

God instructed the Israelites to call the worship place a sanctuary or holy place because it was a place where the holy God would dwell. It was also a place where God's people would carry out a holy purpose—worship. The people would be represented in worship by holy people or priests.

God alone is holy within himself. He is the only one who could establish the holy nature of the worship place and personnel that would serve in it. In these verses God promised to do just that. "Consecrate" (29:43–44) is the verb from which the noun "sanctuary" is derived. To consecrate something or to make it holy meant to remove it from the normal sphere of life and reserve it exclusively for the use of God. God shared detailed instructions about the ceremony that should be carried out in order to conse-crate the priests and the tabernacle, including its furniture. Ultimately, however, God himself (his glory) rather than the rituals accomplished the act of consecration.

All Christians should understand the responsibility of using some of their hard-earned income to make possible a place to worship God.

God promised them that when they worshiped through bringing their sacrifices to him, he would "meet" them (29:43). This word contains the idea of an appointment. Worship is important because it is keeping an appointment that God has made with us.

The "altar" (29:44) built of acacia wood overlaid with bronze was positioned in the courtyard (27:1–8). God selected "Aaron and his sons" (29:44) to serve as priests. Priests represented the people before God (offering sacrifices) and represented God to the people (giving instruction). The Israelites carried out these instructions later (Leviticus 8).

A consecrated priesthood serving in a consecrated sanctuary would make possible the dwelling of God among the people. "Dwell" (Exod. 29:45–46) is the same word found in Exodus 25:8. God had delivered the Israelites from Egyptian slavery and brought them to himself at Sinai. Now, through the worship place that God provided them, he would accompany them when they left Sinai. Their worship of God would be a continual reminder of the great things God had done for them.

> *The only reason that we have gifts to share with God is that God gives them to us.*

The Will of God (33:7–11, 14–16)

While God gave Moses instructions for the building of the tabernacle (Exod. 25—31), God's people worshiped God in an unacceptable way (32:1–6). God determined to punish them instead of destroy them, and then God pondered what to do with them beyond that (33:1–6). They needed some direction from God. They needed to know God's will for their future. In other words they needed to experience God's presence.

Priesthood of All Believers

The priesthood of all believers is a keystone belief among Baptists. We believe that Jesus is the greatest Priest and only Mediator between humanity and God. We believe that our position as followers of Christ makes all of us priests. This belief gives freedom-loving Baptists the privilege of enjoying equal access to God and ultimate accountability only to God. No other authority whether church or creed or convention has a rightful place between God and us.

We have equal access to the Scriptures. We are responsible for interpreting their meaning for our lives. We have equal responsibility in ministry. We do not possess the same kind of giftedness, but we are each responsible to use our giftedness in serving others.

This doctrine is frightening to some people because it appears to grant too much individuality or independence. It is at that point that we must trust the Holy Spirit who lives within each of us to guide us in being the priest that we ought to be.

The "tent of meeting" (33:7) met those needs. When anyone needed to seek an answer from the Lord or to know the Lord's will concerning a particular matter, the person made it known to Moses. Moses would then represent the seeker before God by entering the tent of meeting. The Israelites would know that God made himself available to meet Moses because "the pillar of cloud would come down and stay at the entrance" (33:9).

Serious communication took place between God and Moses. The Israelites used "face to face" (33:11) as an idiom of intimacy. It signified the reality and depth of communion between Moses and the Lord. God honored those who would seek him and know his will. The people respected the fact that God shared himself with them in order to provide guidance for them (33:10). Experiencing God's presence and knowing God's response would result in "rest" (33:14) or wholeness, security. Moses correctly understood that the presence of God in Israel was the feature that distinguished them from all other peoples (33:16).

God instructed the Israelites to call the worship place a sanctuary or holy place because it was a place where the holy God would dwell.

God in his grace offers us the privilege of Christian worship. We are granted the opportunity of approaching the holy God in ways God chooses. Among the important reasons that we desire to experience God's presence in worship is to learn more about him and to listen to him. We need to know God's will and purpose for our lives. In individual as well as corporate worship experiences we discover that will.

The Glory of God (40:16–38)

Understanding the biblical witness concerning worship structures in the Exodus and wilderness period is not an easy task. It is true that the term "tent of meeting" is the same phrase found both in Exodus 33:7 and 29:44 and that the tent described in Exodus 28—29 is the tabernacle with courtyard prescribed in this book. The terms are completely interchangeable in Exodus 40. On the other hand, the descriptions of the tent of meeting and tabernacle show some obvious differences. Numbers 2 uses both terms—tent of meeting and tabernacle—and describes the structure as being positioned at the center of the camp. In Exodus 33:7, the tent

Why?

You have agreed with the president of your service organization to host an exchange student for several months. She is a bright and articulate college student from a country in southeast Asia. She has no background or previous experience whatsoever with Christian faith or worship.

After the first Sunday of attending church with your family, she takes the worship guide and says, "I need to ask you some things about this morning." What are the things (building, setting, activities) that you believe she would be curious about? What would your answers be?

---

was situated "outside the camp." The tent of meeting seems to have been a simpler structure in contrast to the more elaborate form and furniture of the tabernacle. While Aaron and his sons served the tabernacle, the tent was guarded by Joshua (33:11).

Puzzled Old Testament commentators come to various conclusions in the interpretation of this biblical evidence. Some assert that the Israelites had only one structure known by several names and possibly passed down through different strands of tradition and memory. Others feel that Moses utilized the tent of meeting either before he received the instructions for the tabernacle or during the interim

We are granted the opportunity of approaching the holy God in ways God chooses.

period of judgment for the golden calf incident. The purposes of the two structures ultimately coalesced. Exodus 40 certainly reflects that coming together.

Moses received God's building plans (Exod. 25—31) but was interrupted by the crisis of the golden calf incident and its resolution (Exod. 32—34). Then Moses proceeded to lead the Israelites in the construction of the tabernacle (Exod. 35—40).

Exodus 40:16–38 provides an executive summary of all the work that had been done. Moses "finished the work" (40:33), doing all of it "just as the LORD commanded him" (40:16). "Finished" translates the same verb that declares the conclusion of the creation event (Genesis 2:1). This summary declared the completion of the construction of

- the framework and covering of the two-room building (Exod. 40:18–19)

- the furniture in those two rooms, including the most holy place (the inner room, 40:20–21), and the holy place (the outer room, "outside the curtain," 40:22–28)
- the furniture placed in the courtyard (40:29–32)
- the enclosure of the courtyard perimeter (40:33)

Again the "cloud" served as the visible reminder that God was present (40:34). When they left Sinai, it served as the sign that God desired them to move on toward the land of promise (40:36–38). The "glory of the LORD" that filled the tabernacle denoted the recognized status, reputation, or influence of God (40:35). This phrase almost became another way to describe the being of God. God had chosen to dwell among his people by being unmistakably with them in that worship place. What a joy it is to gather with God's people in worship and together experience the awesome presence of God.

> *What a joy it is to gather with God's people in worship and together experience the awesome presence of God.*

This portable sanctuary or tabernacle has been examined and studied extensively. Some biblical interpreters find a measure of significance or hidden meaning (allegory) in the smallest details of dimension, color schemes, and furniture relationships. I am not as comfortable as some are in drawing such conclusions.

The New Testament itself pays little attention to the tabernacle except in the Book of Hebrews. What we can be confident of is that while the tabernacle was the place where God chose to dwell among his people during that time, God ultimately chose to dwell among us in God's Son, Jesus. In John 1:14 the statement that the Word "made his dwelling among us" includes the word for *tabernacled* or *pitched his tent*. Since God dwells with us in Jesus, we who trust in Jesus can express God's dwelling with us eternally (see Revelation 21:3).

QUESTIONS

1. Study the worship center in your church as to its architectural design, the windows, and the pieces and arrangement of furnishings. What statements about God do you detect?

2. Study the worship services in your church. What role does each element in the service play in getting people in touch with God?

3. What are the major reasons some Christians do not give consistently according to biblical standards? What can or should the church do about that?

4. How do we preserve some sense of the holiness of God when we worship and thereby prevent our worship from being mere entertainment?

5. When have you gained some understanding or direction from God about a matter in your life during a time of worship? Did you follow that direction? Why or why not?

6. Participation in worship is keeping a scheduled appointment with God. How do you prepare properly for these important times?

2 CORINTHIANS:
Taking Ministry Personally

UNIT ONE, MINISTERING TO PEOPLE WHO DISAGREE

Lesson 1	When You Suffer	2 Corinthians 1:1–11
Lesson 2	When Relationships Are Strained	2 Corinthians 1:12—2:11
Lesson 3	Measuring Our Ministry	2 Corinthians 2:14—3:6
Lesson 4	Maintaining Heart for Ministry	2 Corinthians 4:1–15
Lesson 5	Confidence for Now and Forever	2 Corinthians 4:16—5:10
Lesson 6	Motivated to Minister	2 Corinthians 5:11–21
Lesson 7	Be Faithful, Be Real	2 Corinthians 6:1–13; 7:2–4
Lesson 8	Giving and Receiving Criticism	2 Corinthians 7:5–16

UNIT TWO, LEARNING TO GIVE

| Lesson 9 | Reasons for Giving | 2 Corinthians 8:1–21 |
| Lesson 10 | Blessings of Giving | 2 Corinthians 9:6–15 |

UNIT THREE, GETTING BEYOND THE STATUS QUO

Lesson 11	Dealing with Conflict	2 Corinthians 10
Lesson 12	Grace Sufficient	2 Corinthians 12:1–10
Lesson 13	On Trying to Change People	2 Corinthians 12:14—13:13

Additional Resources for Studying 2 Corinthians[1]

Paul Barnett. *The Second Epistle to the Corinthians.* The New International Commentary on the New Testament. Grand Rapids, Michigan: William B. Eerdmans Publishing Company, 1997.

G.R. Beasley-Murray. "2 Corinthians." *The Broadman Bible Commentary.* Volume 11. Nashville, Tennessee: Broadman Press, 1971.

Ernest Best. *Second Corinthians.* Interpretation: A Bible Commentary for Teaching and Preaching. Louisville: John Knox Press, 1987.

F.F. Bruce. *1 and 2 Corinthians.* New Century Bible. London: Oliphants, 1971.

Kenneth L. Chafin. *1, 2 Corinthians.* The Communicator's Commentary. Waco, Texas: Word Books, Publisher, 1985.

David Garland. *2 Corinthians.* The New American Commentary. Nashville, Tennessee: Broadman and Holman, 1999.

Brian Harbour. *2 Corinthians: Commissioned to Serve.* Nashville, Tennessee: Convention Press, 1989.

John B. Polhill. *Paul and His Letters.* Nashville, Tennessee: Broadman and Holman Publishers, 1999.

A.T. Robertson. *Word Pictures in the New Testament.* Volume IV. Nashville, Tennessee: Broadman Press, 1931.

J. Paul Sampley. "The Second Letter to the Corinthians." *The New Interpreter's Bible.* Volume XI. Nashville: Abingdon Press, 2000.

NOTES

1. Listing a book does not imply full agreement by the writers or BAPTISTWAY PRESS® with all of its comments.

How to Order More Bible Study Materials

It's easy! Just fill in the following information. (Note: when the *Teaching Guide* is priced at $1.95, the *Teaching Guide* contains only teaching plans.)✦ = Texas specific

Title of item	Price	Quantity	Cost
This Issue:			
Exodus: Freed to Follow God—Study Guide	$2.35	_____	_____
Exodus: Freed to Follow God—Large Print Study Guide	$2.35	_____	_____
Exodus: Freed to Follow God—Teaching Guide	$2.95	_____	_____
Previous Issues Available:			
God's Message in the Old Testament—Study Guide✦	$1.95	_____	_____
God's Message in the Old Testament—Teaching Guide✦	$1.95	_____	_____
Genesis 12—50: Family Matters—Study Guide	$1.95	_____	_____
Genesis 12—50: Family Matters—Large Print Study Guide	$1.95	_____	_____
Genesis 12—50: Family Matters—Teaching Guide	$2.45	_____	_____
Isaiah and Jeremiah—Study Guide	$1.95	_____	_____
Isaiah and Jeremiah—Large Print Study Guide	$1.95	_____	_____
Isaiah and Jeremiah—Teaching Guide	$2.45	_____	_____
Amos, Hosea, Micah—Study Guide	$1.95	_____	_____
Amos, Hosea, Micah—Teaching Guide	$2.45	_____	_____
Good News in the New Testament—Study Guide✦	$1.95	_____	_____
Good News in the New Testament—Large Print Study Guide✦	$1.95	_____	_____
Good News in the New Testament—Teaching Guide✦	$2.45	_____	_____
Matthew: Jesus As the Fulfillment of God's Promises—Study Guide✦	$1.00	_____	_____
Matthew: Jesus As the Fulfillment of God's Promises—Large Print Study Guide✦	$1.00	_____	_____
Matthew: Jesus As the Fulfillment of God's Promises—Teaching Guide✦	$2.00	_____	_____
Jesus in the Gospel of Mark—Study Guide	$1.95	_____	_____
Jesus in the Gospel of Mark—Large Print Study Guide	$1.95	_____	_____
Jesus in the Gospel of Mark—Teaching Guide	$2.45	_____	_____
Luke: Parables Jesus Told—Study Guide	$2.35	_____	_____
Luke: Parables Jesus Told—Large Print Study Guide	$2.35	_____	_____
Luke: Parables Jesus Told—Teaching Guide	$2.95	_____	_____
Gospel of John—Study Guide	$1.95	_____	_____
Gospel of John—Large Print Study Guide	$1.95	_____	_____
Gospel of John—Teaching Guide	$2.45	_____	_____
Acts: Sharing God's Good News with Everyone—Study Guide✦	$1.95	_____	_____
Acts: Sharing God's Good News with Everyone—Teaching Guide✦	$1.95	_____	_____
Romans: Good News for a Troubled World—Study Guide✦	$1.95	_____	_____
Romans: Good News for a Troubled World—Teaching Guide✦	$1.95	_____	_____
1 Corinthians—Study Guide	$1.95	_____	_____
1 Corinthians—Large Print Study Guide	$1.95	_____	_____
1 Corinthians—Teaching Guide	$2.45	_____	_____
Galatians and Ephesians—Study Guide✦	$1.95	_____	_____
Galatians and Ephesians—Large Print Study Guide✦	$1.95	_____	_____
Galatians and Ephesians—Teaching Guide✦	$2.45	_____	_____
Philippians, Colossians, Thessalonians—Teaching Guide	$2.45	_____	_____
Hebrews and James—Study Guide	$1.95	_____	_____
Hebrews and James—Large Print Study Guide	$1.95	_____	_____
Hebrews and James—Teaching Guide	$2.45	_____	_____
Letters of John and Peter—Study Guide	$1.95	_____	_____
Letters of John and Peter—Large Print Study Guide	$1.95	_____	_____
Letters of John and Peter—Teaching Guide	$2.45	_____	_____

Coming for use beginning September 2004

2 Corinthians: Taking Ministry Personally—Study Guide	$2.35	
2 Corinthians: Taking Ministry Personally—Large Print Study Guide	$2.35	
2 Corinthians: Taking Ministry Personally—Teaching Guide	$2.95	

Beliefs Important to Baptists

Who in the World Are Baptists, Anyway? (one lesson)	$ .45	
Who in the World Are Baptists, Anyway?—Teacher's Edition	$ .55	
Beliefs Important to Baptists: I (four lessons)	$1.35	
Beliefs Important to Baptists: I—Teacher's Edition	$1.75	
Beliefs Important to Baptists: II (four lessons)	$1.35	
Beliefs Important to Baptists: II—Teacher's Edition	$1.75	
Beliefs Important to Baptists: III (four lessons)	$1.35	
Beliefs Important to Baptists: III—Teacher's Edition	$1.75	
Beliefs Important to Baptists—Study Guide (one-volume edition; includes all lessons)	$2.35	
Beliefs Important to Baptists—Teaching Guide (one-volume edition; includes all lessons)	$1.95	

*Charges for standard shipping service:

Subtotal up to $20.00	$3.95
Subtotal $20.01—$50.00	$4.95
Subtotal $50.01—$100.00	10% of subtotal
Subtotal $100.01 and up	8% of subtotal

Please allow three weeks for standard delivery. For express shipping service: Call 1–866–249–1799 for information on additional charges.

Subtotal _____

Shipping* _____

TOTAL _____

Your name _____ Phone _____

Your church _____ Date Ordered _____

Mailing address _____

City _____ State _____ Zip code _____

MAIL this form with your check for the total amount to
BAPTISTWAY PRESS
Baptist General Convention of Texas
333 North Washington
Dallas, TX 75246-1798
(Make checks to "Baptist Executive Board.")

OR, **FAX** your order anytime to: 214-828-5187, and we will bill you.

OR, **CALL** your order toll-free: 1-866-249-1799 (8:30 a.m.-5:00 p.m., M-F), and we will bill you.

OR, **E-MAIL** your order to our internet e-mail address: baptistway@bgct.org, and we will bill you.

We look forward to receiving your order! Thank you!